INSIDE
SILICON
VALLEY

INSIDE SILICON VALLEY

How the deals get done

MARC PHILLIPS

M
MELBOURNE BOOKS

Published by Melbourne Books
Level 9, 100 Collins Street,
Melbourne, VIC 3000
Australia
www.melbournebooks.com.au
info@melbournebooks.com.au

National Library of Australia
Cataloguing-in-Publication entry (pbk)
Author: Phillips, Marc.
Title: Inside Silicon Valley : How the deals get done.
ISBN: 9781922129185 (paperback)
Subjects: Success in business--California.
Computer industry--California--Santa Clara Valley
(Santa Clara County)
Microelectronics industry--California--Santa Clara
Valley (Santa Clara County)
Santa Clara Valley (Santa Clara County, Calif.)--
Economicconditions.
Dewey Number: 658.8009794

Previous books by Marc Philips:
Successful e-Commerce
The World's Best Online Advertising Campaigns

Luck follows the brave in Silicon Valley.
Come here, tell your story, they will listen.

With heartfelt thanks to:
Gene de Rose, Drew Ianni, Andrew Tymms, Cameron Yuill,
Joe Kennedy, Gower Smith, Gary Ireland, Jose Suarez,
Graeme Marsh and David Tenenbaum.

Dedicated to:
Anneliese and Cassie for Friday Morning pancakes
at Ann's Coffee Shop in Menlo Park CA.

Author's Note

I first came to Silicon Valley from Australia in 2000 after the acquisition of my Australian online software company. I intended to stay a few weeks to chance my hand at raising capital for a new venture....and ended up making it my home. I expected a high paced, high tech, cut throat environment, but what I found was quite the opposite...a supportive, folksy community that embraces those who make a commitment to following their dreams and residing in the Valley.

After being involved in various successful start ups, I am now also a partner in a Venture Capital firm and it is from the perspective gained of being both an entrepreneur and VC that I write this book.

The book is a road map of how to go about pursuing your dream of raising capital, how to format an investment presentation and practical real life tips to avoid mistakes made by start-up founders.

Drawing on my personal experiences, I give insights into the mechanics of this unique community of venture capitalists and entrepreneurs and what really goes on Inside Silicon Valley.

Marc Phillips
2013
www.arafuraventures.com

Contents

INTRODUCTION
THE BILLIONAIRE'S FACTORY

The foyer at Sequoia Capital, arguably the most pre-eminent venture capital firm in Silicon Valley, at 3000 Sand Hill Road, Menlo Park, has a wall-mounted television screen displaying sliding profile pictures of the founders of Atari, Cisco, Oracle, Apple, Google, YouTube and LinkedIn. As I sat there waiting I realized that Sequoia were pretty darn good at picking start-up companies to invest in. For those of us here in Silicon Valley, it's like sitting outside Steven Spielberg's office wondering if you're going to get a part in his next blockbuster.

Situated next to the Sharon Heights Golf Club, Sequoia's office is the last exit before the Interstate 280 as you head down Sand Hill Road. The beautiful redwood trees climb up past the floor-to-ceiling glass windows and the serenity of being in the tree-lined cul-de-sac is interrupted by the receptionist, who asks, 'Would you please come this way?'

It's April 2008 and for the first time I was bringing in a deal to a meeting at Sequoia with three partners present. A full partner meeting would make the final decision on the $6 million Series A investment on a mobile payments company that I was helping raise money for.

Getting an appointment for most entrepreneurs with a Sand Hill

Road venture capitalist (VC) is in itself a challenging task. That's because most outsiders find it very difficult to get a referral — which is how, 99 percent of the time, VCs agree to take meetings with start-ups looking to raise money. To be taken seriously you have to be introduced by a 'friend of the firm', and by that I mean someone connected with one of their portfolio companies or friend of a mutual professional colleague.

I'd been introduced to Mark Kvamme, a well-known partner of Sequoia Capital back in 2006, by Drew Ianni who runs APPNATION Conference. Drew had worked for Kvamme at CKS Interactive 'back in the day' (which means in the dot-com bubble of the 1990s). Mark's father, Floyd Kvamme, is a partner emeritus at Kleiner Perkins Caulfield & Byers, the old-school establishment venture capital firm in Silicon Valley. As a board member of LinkedIn and other notable start-ups that were household names amongst Silicon Valley folks, I was excited to meet Mark.

VCs are very time-efficient. The ethos is not to waste an entrepreneur's time and, in the most part, they totally admire that an entrepreneur would risk it all to work and build something that may change the world. It's normal practice for a VC to have the entrepreneur set up their laptop prior to them entering the board or meeting room so that when they sit down the entrepreneurs can commence the PowerPoint presentation pitch or the hardware/ software demonstration without unnecessary delay.

This was the second time that Kvamme had heard the investment pitch, but this time the two other Sequoia partners had not. I'd let Mark know that the founder had family responsibilities to return to and, if they were interested in investing, we needed a fast answer. Mark obliged by setting up this second meeting for the following day.

VCs will bring in one and possibly two other partners when

they ask an entrepreneur back to re-pitch. It's their way of getting the deal sponsored internally. Most VCs do this before they put their suggested companies up for formal approval at the fortnightly partners' meeting. Not all venture firms are this structured, but the larger ones tend to have regular meetings where all the partners present their favored deals to one another.

As Roelof Botha, who had been CFO of PayPal and now a Sequoia partner who had served on the board of YouTube, together with Gaurav Garg, also a Sequoia partner, sat and listened, I noticed the sweat on the brow of the founder. Not a good sign. I glanced at Mark Kvamme and he was as relaxed as ever, graciously trying to create a relaxed environment for the CEO pitching.

VCs, like most financiers, feel you out as their prey. They look at you in a way that makes you uncomfortable and the body language can pierce the toughest armor of a company founder. The meeting lasted the obligatory 60 minutes, with the VCs taking a deep dive into the financial forecasts and go to market slides in the presentation.

It's all about scale for VCs, and by that I mean how fast and steep the hockey stick of growth can be. As they calibrated the last month's and quarter's growth rates of customer acquisition and quizzed the founder on milestones, you could hear the gears inside their heads crunching the numbers. This wasn't only about what they thought the technology; it was about how exponential the growth of adoption was. That's what Google, YouTube, LinkedIn had: massive adoption at faster rates than their competitors. That's what VCs want, so ultimately they can IPO or trade sale based on the exponential growth. My mind flashed to their $11.5 million investment in YouTube and the $1.65 billion sale to Google.

They huddled outside the meeting room for ten minutes while I, the CEO and CTO of the mobile/social payments software company, sat looking out at the line of Mercedes, Porsches and BMWs in the car park. These guys were about to decide the future of these two founders. It happens in a blink of an eye!

Mark and Roelof returned to the room and said, 'We're going to pass.' Just like that. It wasn't, 'Thanks for coming in, we'll let you know'; it was more sudden and final than that. The saying in Silicon Valley from VCs is 'a quick no is a good no', as it preserves their integrity and lets the start-up executives move on quickly, despite the initial disappointment. Sequoia are true professionals in their trade.

Part of their reason was the adoption of payments on mobile, incumbent competition and mostly the speed at which the viral adoption of the software by users would take place. I asked, 'How do you tell if a start-up is going to go viral like a PayPal or a LinkedIn?' They both looked at me, smiled and answered, 'We don't. That's the scary part of what we do.'

As we piled out of the Sequoia Capital offices with the images of the television screen blinking at us, I took a photo of the entrepreneurs outside and emailed it to them. In time, they'll hopefully remember the experience as a reminder of how few grace these offices and leave with commitment of an investment.

Incidentally, the business was called Mobillcash which was acquired by Boku in June 2009. Boku has raised $73M in venture capital (*www.crunchbase.com/company/boku*).

As I turned off my bed light I looked out my window to the climbing twisted branches of the California oaks outside my house, reflected on the day and thought that many entrepreneurs don't even get to meet with partners of a venture capital firm like Sequoia Capital, let alone have a company growing fast enough to secure a full partner meeting.

It's a reminder of how hard it can be to make it in Silicon Valley and the serendipitous nature of start-ups.

1

BEFORE THE PITCH

The Golden Rolodex Promise

Just about all entrepreneurs have looked at the Sand Hill Road venture capital websites (Sequoia Capital, Benchmark Ventures, Khosla Ventures, to name a few) and read the biographies of managing partners who have taken companies public or sold for hundreds of millions. The promise on many Silicon Valley venture capital websites is that they come with a 'golden rolodex' of contacts — insiders and influencers, the right people to meet both socially and, more importantly, professionally to fast-track your start-up company's growth.

In May 2007, as Tim Guleri, Managing Partner of Sierra Ventures (a \$1 billion+ venture fund located on Sand Hill Road), and I were heading south on the Interstate 280 to Yahoo! in Santa Clara, I remember thinking, 'This guy is the real deal.' Tim had arranged a meeting with John Galatea, Vice President of Sales, and Dustin Suchter, a sales engineer, both with Yahoo! They were kind enough to accept a meeting to review some technology in the search sector. The ability to give entrepreneurs access to executives offers kudos to VCs. The meeting went well with John and Dustin, providing me and Tim with commercial feedback on the viability of the search technology solution.

This is how good VCs conduct due diligence and is a great way for entrepreneurs to meet potential partners and eventual acquirers of their technology.

Driving out of the Yahoo! offices, I parked just off Great America Parkway in Santa Clara and noticed lots of people praying on the lawn in front of the 40-foot statute of Mary towering over the US Interstate 101. There's a lot of praying in Silicon Valley, and not only by entrepreneurs. VCs provide value, direction and a good ear, but often they are not in control and really would be better off praying for their portfolio companies.

The most important point to understand if you're an entrepreneur is that, inside the Valley, there's an unspoken agreement between VCs and corporate executives. That is, for the advice and analysis given by the executives, the VC will keep them in mind for future job opportunities. Most executives in Silicon Valley are not working for the pay packet. It's presumed that their base compensation is the opportunity cost of not working in a start-up themselves and their stock option package, which typically vests over four years on a quarterly in-arrears basis, is the 'upside' that executives are really working for. That's how real money is made. That's an each-way bet on how to get rich. Pay the bills and the options convert when the company's common stock is at a much higher price.

This is a good thing. It's the quid pro quo or payback for executives helping each other. When executives are thinking of jumping from one company to another, they often reach out to VCs and ask for any openings in hot start-up companies. That's how it rolls here in the Valley. Not too different from most parts of the world, but here it's more orchestrated. It's part of the mechanics and is well understood. You help a VC do the due diligence and they'll help get you into a hot company they are funding if the opportunity arises.

It even goes deeper than that. If a VC is thinking of funding a company, they might do so on the proviso that an executive they like becomes part of the team. It's a well-oiled employment production machine.

Silicon Valley can be a lonely place for entrepreneurs. It's akin to a nightclub when you're first going out socially. You're young, want to look good and act smart, but there are always cooler guys and better-looking girls. So, when someone takes an interest in you personally and you *get it* (Silicon Valley parlance for understanding their business model or technology), then they often befriend you.

It's important for entrepreneurs to realize that mentorship is at best, in my opinion, hollow promises that often come at a steep price. The right way to structure an advisor role in your company is to provide 0.25 to one percent of the stock option pool to an advisor over 18 to 24 months. I think four years is too long, as advisors are good for a short burst in start-ups, and as the business grows you need other people with broader skill sets.

Mentors are great for young kids fresh out of college and new to the Bay Area. But, they are not needed when you're older. I know of several accelerators in Silicon Valley that take too much for their mentorship. They take five to ten percent of founders' common stock and then give $200,000 to $250,000 in an uncapped convertible note. That's good for the investor but not so good for entrepreneurs. My advice is to find mentors elsewhere.

Take heed in the words of Gordon Gecko from Wall Street: 'If you need a friend, get a dog.' Because in Silicon Valley, dogs have hotels, they go to work with their owners, and generally are great social initiators to get you talking to other people in parks. You're just as likely to meet someone that can help you while you're walking your dog as you are giving up five to ten percent to tech mentors who order in lunch everyday and wave their hands in front of PowerPoint presentations.

Be wary of mentors and mentorship programs. They prey on the inexperienced with their so-called intellectual capital or value capital. Look for VCs that add value and make introductions even before they invest. That's your due diligence as much as it is theirs. VCs like Tim Guleri listen intently, don't promise mentorship but rather get into the field with entrepreneurs and take them to market as part of the investment process — which is great for entrepreneurs who want real feedback from experienced people.

Forget the promise of the VC's golden rolodex. What is important is their managing partners' willingness to make introductions. My advice is to pick one like Tim who has sold his company for several hundred millions of dollars before becoming a VC.

What's My Start-up Worth?

Valuation is not as hard as you think. It's an inevitable question that VCs will ask entrepreneurs and one that I know often pains the start-up guys. The way most Silicon Valley VCs like to hear it is that you're going to arrive at a valuation for them to reasonably be able to calculate a minimum 10x return on their money. Remember, venture capital is high-risk investment. The bigger VCs, like Sequoia, Accel Partners and Benchmark Ventures, live for their 500x return on investments. Think: Google, eBay and Facebook as companies that have *return on investment* multiples 200 to 500 times the initial investments.

Living in Palo Alto, I've seen many *friends and family* deals get done by neighbors and college alumni. It's typical for a $100,000–150,000 seed investment to be syndicated out to five to ten seed investors at between $10,000 and $20,000 per investor. That's enough for two people to quit their jobs to work on their software start-up full-time for six months, just enough to cover what they would have been paid if they were still working in their corporate job.

'First-in' investors typically want a 2–3x return or *uptick* on their invested money. In Silicon Valley as private investors, it is expected that, on the next valuation, their shares are worth two to three times more. For example, if the $100,000 is raised at a valuation of $1 million, then the investors would hope that the next investment round will be between $2 million to $3 million.

The smarter seed or angel investors want to have between five and ten percent if they write a check for up to $100,000. It's often for a chunk of a company that is little more than an idea, a very basic demo or alpha software that isn't even built or demonstrable to prospective customers.

By the time you get your software start-up to professional angel investors or 'smart money' (the VCs who understand the market and have strategic connections), the metrics behind a valuation need to be understood. You're not asking your parents or friends for money. You're swimming with sharks now.

Working from the previous example, you've given up ten percent for $100,000 at a valuation of $1 million. To be exact, that's a 'post-money valuation' of $1 million and it's a pre-money valuation of $900,000. It's better to include a pre-money valuation in the pitch deck, as it's a lower number and looks sweeter to potential investors.

It is very important that entrepreneurs understand the difference between pre-money and post-money valuations. Often, angle investors will say to an entrepreneur, 'You don't need to raise $1 million — so what is the valuation if you raise only $750,000?' Savvy investors will ask these questions to determine how flexible the valuation is. It's a cunning way for investors to test your resolve on valuation and what propensity you have to negotiate.

Nonetheless, Silicon Valley venture capital needs their billionaire founders. Like movie stars, the Valley needs pin-up poster kids that rake in hundreds of millions of dollars. They are the tangible examples of what Silicon Valley is to entrepreneurs, that the promise of venture capital pays off for everyone involved.

Today, with online news beats like *TechCrunch*, Vator, Crunchbase and Wikipedia recording the acquisition prices and how many shares of a public company a founder was issued, it's easier to calculate the worth of the founders in exits. As a rule of thumb, VCs typically like to see the founders of a company ending up with between ten and 15 percent each after two or three rounds of funding.

Here is an example. Say you're looking at a $1.5 million Series A after raising $100,000 in seed capital. You may value your company at a pre-money valuation of $4.5 million. This means you're going to give up around 25 percent, which translates to a post-valuation of $6 million. Most importantly, the next round of funding gives you 12 to 18 months of *financial runway* (Silicon Valley speak for the length of time you have to burn through the money) and allows you to build a team, release more enhanced versions of the software, and execute on sales and distribution.

The Series B valuation can move into a much larger amount, between $10 million and $20 million, depending on how fast you are growing and how capital-intensive the company is. Again, the Series B valuation will want to see the VC take an additional 15 to 25 percent of the company. All the time, the VC is looking at how they can turn their investment into a 10– 20x return at a minimum.

As the Series C and D rounds of venture capital take place, the higher valuation ensures that the founders' and previous shareholders' equity value increases. If the company isn't able to raise money at a higher valuation than the previous round of capital, it is known as a *down round*. If the company raises money at the same valuation as previous rounds, it is referred to as a *flat round* because the valuation is the same.

My overall advice to entrepreneurs is: don't overly concern yourselves with your start-up company valuation because, if it succeeds, your founding stock will be worth more money than you could ever really spend.

I've seen VCs shut down companies that they have invested tens of millions of dollars into because it would not provide the internal rates of return that they wish to show their investors. I'm serious. Silicon Valley venture funds will kill a company if they don't believe it will ever return the multiples of investment, or when they lose faith in the management team or the business model becomes unstable. This happened to a Los Angeles–based start-up technology company called Geodelic. As an advisor and shareholder for four years, Geodelic raised $600,000 in seed capital, and $3.1 million in Series A and $6 million in Series B from notable VCs such as Shasta Ventures, Clearstone Venture Partners, MK Capital and Verizon Ventures. Geodelic went from being a mobile app that merchants like Universal Studios and Carl's Jr. fast food stores could brand as their own location-based app, to a platform for telcos to enable mobile deals for their retail customers. In hindsight, you could say there were too many *pivots* (a Silicon Valley term to describe the changing product and business models a technology start-up company has). Valuations at seed round, Series A and Series B proved worthless, given the VCs would not fund the company into a Series C round and, as such, Geodelic eventually closed down.

While business models morph, there needs to be a consistency of revenue model through the various rounds of funding in order to maximize valuation and funding opportunities.

Remember that valuations are arbitrary before a company is sold. You can have a great valuation on Series A of $10 million and Series B of $30 million, and if the company fails then everyone's shareholding is worth zero.

BEING INVESTMENT-READY

You can tell pretty quickly by looking at the emails from start-up founders if they are *investment-ready*. I suggest to entrepreneurs to only send the investment presentation to VCs. I believe that multiple attachments in emails are confusing and overwhelming to VCs. Entrepreneurs should hold back letters of intent, white papers, press articles and Excel spreadsheets with complex financials in the first initial communications with VCs. Keep it simple; keep it to the investment presentation.

It is really easy for young entrepreneurs to mess up during VC meetings and phone calls. A light-hearted story illustrates where one young entrepreneur I know by the name of Eric didn't have the attention to detail. He was meeting some of us at the Dutch Goose, (*www.dutchgoose.net*) which is located on Alameda de las Pulgas in Menlo Park, minutes from Sand Hill Road. It's a local drinking hole for Stanford alumni and the locals. He decided to take the Friday afternoon call from the car he'd parked outside the pub. When he entered the Goose, his face was blank. To his dismay, he seriously messed up. The GoToMeeting (*www.gotomeeting.com*) hadn't been downloaded onto the boardroom computer at the San Francisco office the VC was visiting for the day. Then, it started raining and the noise from the raindrops bouncing off the car roof was almost deafening. Johan had switched to Skype in the car, yet the echoing on a three-way conference call via Skype (he'd patched in another VC who was in another location) meant one of the other VCs had to hang up.

What a disaster. Therein lies the lesson: entrepreneurs should be prepared for every communications hiccup. You should make it easy on the VC. Don't assume that VCs will be viewing the presentation on their computer or they will have the GoToMeeting desktop application installed onto their computer. Even if you've sent an email with instructions, don't assume they will have it ready. They should, but it can ruin your life if they don't! You get one shot at some of these VCs — one phone call. Don't ring from the car; you're not ordering pizza!

Don't use Skype, either. The voice quality is inconsistent, and patching people into a conference call can lead to having one person dropping off. The Skype screen-sharing function hogs up the CPU on your computer, which can cripple the voice quality and, on some machines, creates a strange noise. People, I'm speaking from personal experience here! During rains and storms here in the Valley, voice over IP (VOIP) quality can deteriorate!

My advice is to send the investment pitch as a PDF via email. It's a small detail but saves everyone time and messing around. This way, it is viewable on any PC, tablet or smartphone (whether iOS or Android).

By sending your investment deck through to the VCs, they can quickly scan it and see that it is professionally laid out, colorful and follows the sequence required in Silicon Valley standard decks. That is the preliminary work. While it's common practice for most VCs to peruse the deck to get an idea of what the business is about, they often don't want to misread it or get the wrong impression, which is why they wait for the entrepreneur to walk through the presentation.

That said, sending it to the VC ensures that you are not doing a live demo using GoToMeeting, WebEx or the free version of Join. me (*www.join.me*), which is a favorite of budget-conscious start-ups. This ensures that, when you get onto the call, you can commence the pitch without unnecessary delay. VCs like to have the entrepreneur dive into the pitch quickly within one or two minutes of the call. They often schedule 30 minutes for the call and state upfront that they have a *hard stop* (a Silicon Valley term to used to predefine the time they have allocated on for the phone call). Being prepared allows you to maximize the time on the call. It also puts the onus on the VCs to have the investment deck open and makes them appreciate that you are prepared and that your time is valuable.

If a product demonstration is part of your presentation, I suggest you be upfront during the call that you'd like to do a short demonstration and ask if the VCs are in front of a computer. You can then email the credentials (web address, username and password) or aaree on a preferred online demo software to use. This way, you have consensus and avoid any technical issue that can stall your presentation mojo.

Lastly, have an elevator pitch. By that, I mean a 15-second pitch. When you're around Silicon Valley, you often meet people in a café or on the street who will introduce you to a colleague they are with. Be ready to respond when they ask, 'What do you do?' Practice your 15-second elevator pitch in the mirror. Go ahead, good-looking, you can do it!

True story: in 2007, I was invited to a Sunday morning breakfast party at a spacious top-storey condo on Pacific Avenue in Pacific Heights, San Francisco. The view overlooking the bay towards the Golden Gate Bridge was spectacular. San Francisco on a clear morning, with endless blue skies into the Pacific Ocean, is just a beautiful site. The usual attorneys were flocking around the start-up founders like seagulls on garlic fries down at Pier 39, the popular San Francisco tourist destination I could see from the terrace. I started chatting with a couple of guys: one lad from England called Pete, and the other, a Finnish guy who introduced himself as Sami. I mentioned how nice the condo was but how difficult it was to find. Remember that, in 2007, Google Maps wasn't as good as it is now. Pete, the British chap, smiled wryly and gave me his card, 'We're going to help solve that problem and make it easy for people to get more information about real estate.' This guy was ready with his 15-second investment pitch. We chatted about technology trends, and as we were standing waiting for the elevator to leave the party I said, 'So what does your company do?' Sami replied, 'We're going to be the best real estate search engine with very rich real estate information.' It was a simple one-liner but it was said with conviction and conveyed a vision. I got in the elevator and looked at the cards of these guys, which said: 'Trulia. Strange name, I thought, but memorable. The founders, Pete

Flint and Sami Inkinen, went on to raise over $30 million in venture capital, and in September 2012 Trulia went public (NYSE: TRLA), raising another $100 million and valuing the company at over $700 million.

I'm sure they used that elevator pitch more than once!

ATTORNEYS AND PAPERWORK

One of the most important pieces of advice I give to entrepreneurs coming to Silicon Valley to raise money is to find an attorney who can do the *paperwork*. The paperwork, in Silicon Valley speak, refers to the term sheet, the incorporation documents, and all related documents and agreements necessary to give the investors comfort that their investment money is going to be protected. The attorney can also provide guidance and counsel to you.

Some of the big names in town are Wilson Sonsini, Cooley, DLA Piper, Fenwick and West and Perkins Coie. These bigger firms have partners at law that will often 'sponsor' a start-up looking to raise money. By this, I mean they will defer their fees. That's right: they'll allow you to meet with them and discuss your business, draft up a term sheet that you as a start-up can give to investors, and even prepare the standard documents for capital-raising. These include the stockholder agreements, stock purchase agreement, employment agreements, investor rights agreements, co-investment agreements and stock option agreements, etc.

If you can pitch an attorney and get them on board to defer fees before going to investors, you're taking the right approach. I've seen attorneys take one to three percent of stock in consideration for doing all Seed round / Series A round documentation with no cash payback on closing of the investment. Yet this is a rare exception. Most of the attorneys will strike a deal where they will punt $25,000 to $40,000 in fees for an agreed period of time — say, six to nine months. The payback of their pre-agreed fees come from the investment dollars raised.

Most importantly, they'll set up an escrow bank account to hold the money that investors deposit into and issue the stockholders agreements for signature and issue stock certificates to investors. This handling of money coming in via checks or electronic bank transfers is crucial to 'closing the deal'.

'When does the deal close?' is a frequent question VCs ask, as they want to know where the deal is in terms of finality. Mustering the investors is a skill akin to herding cats, and creating a sense of urgency for investors to make a decision is crucial.

Attorney offices are neutral territory. If you are a start-up, I think it's a good idea to meet with VCs at attorney offices. DLA Piper at 2000 University Avenue and Perkins Coie on Page Mill Road, Palo Alto, have been the meeting places for many budding start-ups I've met with. If you're a start-up company, it's great positioning meeting investors at an attorney's office space as it affords you an aura of professionalism. I've also seen start-ups bring the attorney into meetings when they are discussing intellectual property and their patent strategy. It's a very smart idea and adds significant weight to the investment pitch.

What start-ups should know is that a good attorney can sit on your board of directors. A typical example would be where you've raised $750,000 from four or five investors. Two of the investors have put in $500,000 and both want a board seat. If there are two founders, they become board members — typically one as chairman/CEO and the other as the president. The attorney can also join the board to act as an impartial member of the team, provide corporate governance advice and provide harmony to the board. I've seen this many times where attorneys smooth the road, provide balanced advice for both investors and entrepreneurs, and in many ways keep the peace.

Being *investment-ready* is critical for raising money in Silicon Valley. This local speak by VCs means that the start-up should not only have their pitch deck in good order but have the paperwork ready. Having a reputable attorney as an aide is very important. It shows investors you're ready to close the investment round.

The gears of a technology investment deal turn faster in Silicon Valley than any other place. Mostly because everyone knows their place. Attorneys produce paperwork that is understood and trusted by venture firms. It's a well-oiled machine that experienced private investors, VCs and the smarter entrepreneurs understand.

Attorneys afford entrepreneurs the professionalism of being able to say with confidence that they are 'closing out the deal in the next few weeks' or 'have a parcel of $100,000 left in the deal before closing'. You don't want to be in a position during a pitch when the investor asks, 'Who is your attorney?' and not have one.

Make the Pitch Entertaining

It is important to flavor your investment presentation with some small dose of entertainment. I'm not talking gimmicks or corny jokes, but rather delivering your pitch deck with a smile, a burst of energy, emphatic tones, perhaps surprise and, where possible, supported with powerful audiovisual appeal in the form of a short (30–60 seconds) video demo to get your audience excited and motivated.

Entrepreneurs are often better equipped for coding rather than telling stories, so if you think your investment pitch is lacking that oomph and engagement factor, I recommend spending a few hours reading a book called *Story* by Robert McKee, who was a professor at the University of Southern California (you might have seen during his cameo in the movie *Adaptation*). *Story* is the screenwriter's bible; it teaches fundamental storytelling techniques.

Perhaps the most entertaining pitch I ever saw was by Rahul Sonnad at Stanford University in August 2010, during the AlwaysOn (*alwayson.goingon.com*) pitch fest. I met Rahul back in 2007, when he was just about to leave thePlatform (*theplatform.com*), which he founded and still remains a leading video management platform for broadband, mobile and TV companies after being acquired by Comcast in June 2006. At Zibbibo restaurant on Kipling Street in Palo Alto, he told me about the idea for Geodelic, a location-based publishing technology allowing mobile operators and enterprises to engage with consumers through flexible offers, rich content and contextual targeting. I became one of the first advisors of the company and over the next four years stayed close to Rahul and the company.

When Rahul was in town from Los Angeles, we'd often head out to The Fillmore, the famous music venue in Korea Town, San Francisco, where all the greats have performed. We enjoyed watching Dave Rawling and Gillian Welch a few times so I knew he loved his folk guitar and bluegrass.

Having raised the Series B of $7 million in June 2010, Rahul was feeling pretty jovial and decided to light up the room of investors at the Knight Management Center at the Stanford Graduate School of Business (GSB) one August afternoon.

Before I tell you what Rahul did that electrified the audience, let me give you an insight into how repetitive a VC's day can be. It's not all high-fives and fist-pumps at exits and IPO parties — 99.9 percent of the time is spent listening to investment pitches that they know before the entrepreneur even enters the room they will say no to. Many times, it's taking the meeting with entrepreneurs because they have been introduced by a mutual colleague, and part of the drill here in Silicon Valley is to uphold protocol and take meetings when one of your respected peers makes an introduction. It's the done thing.

This is often a disheartening aspect of a VC's job and, despite the yearning and enthusiasm to learn and help start-ups, there is a limit to the excitement that even the most optimistic VC can exhale. So it's important to enamor them with some humor, demonstrate your natural ability to hold an audience, tell your story and at the same time entertain.

As Rahul shuffled onto the low-rise stage I'd guesstimate there were 150 people in the room, mostly investors. It was a serious setting. It was Stanford GSB, after all, and AlwaysOn is a top-shelf event, more so than other pitch days in the Valley, mainly because Tony Perkins is an experienced hand at organizing these shows as well as being a venture partner with DFJ Frontier. The morning had been filled with start-ups pitching and Rahul had the session after lunch, when most people are feeling a little worn out and reaching for their fourth cup of coffee for the day.

I was sitting next to Vince Thompson, another advisor to Geodelic, about 15 rows back in the crowd. To our amazement, Rahul stood up and, in broken English and with a heavy Indian accent, muttered into the microphone: 'I am Rahuuul and Gee-Gee-Geodelic is a location-based tech-tech-technology with multifaceted white label.' He paused and the crowd fell into that awkward silence when you know something is terribly wrong or someone is really embarrassing themselves publicly. The crowd had one thought: this guy can't speak English; what the heck is he doing up on stage at AlwaysOn at Stanford!

Rahul wiped his forehead, gulped for air and nervously mumbled the words again. 'Gee-Gee-Geodelic is a location-based platform for mo-mo-mobile carrier for business solutions and white label. We want to deliver audience to know how brand and company can reach consumer with offer ...'

Oh dear, the uncomfortable silence was now disturbed by several people who got up to leave. Oh jeez, what next, the room was silent. I laughed under my breath; he was up to something. Rahul stopped speaking, put his hand to his forehead to get a better look at the two people scurrying out the back door. The tension in the room grew a little and then, with his left hand, he pulled out a ukulele from under the rostrum and stopped and smiled.

The audience were now on the edge of their seat and brimming with the sense you get when you know a performance is about to take place.

Rahul had done what Robert McKee teaches screenwriters to do. He had the audience in a suspended state of reality. They wanted to believe there was going to be something exciting. He had executed on the 'setup' component and was about to deliver a powerful 'payoff' that would see him receive a standing ovation and raucous applause.

Before he even started his song, he had made the pitch entertaining.

Rahul strummed his ukulele and sang a humorously worded tech takeoff of the hit song about Geodelic to the tune of Gloria Gaynor's 'I Will Survive'. The PowerPoint presentation synced to his audio and it reached epic heights when Autumn Radtke, Vice President of Business Development of Geodelic, was pictured showing Sergey Brin, founder of the Google. That's the kind of access start-ups dream of!

The crowd started whooping. Rahul cranked up the volume, eased into a stance reminiscent of Eddie Vedder (the lead singer of Pearl Jam) and finished singing the humorous tune about how Geodelic had survived the twists and turns in mobile innovation and avoided larger competitors.

The audience stood up and clapped Rahul like he was a rock star. I think it was more about him breaking through with a form of entertainment to convey the Geodelic story than giving another stock-standard pitch.

Twenty-five investors stage-tackled Rahul while the audience yelled, 'Encore! Encore!' You can see a video of Rahul performing at *vimeo.com/9567135*.

Therein lies the lesson. The Valley is full of the most interesting people in the world. It really is. Not a week goes by that you don't meet someone with a skill set of world standard, usually from a different part of the world, bringing unique approaches. Entertainment value in investment pitches can make you stand out in this valley of smart people. I hope this story helps you think not only about how to infuse your investment presentation with pizzazz, but also about how to do so for your workplace.

Hollywood is not the only place in California where the words 'The show must go on' is revered.

Forget the Hockey Stick, It's Near Vertical

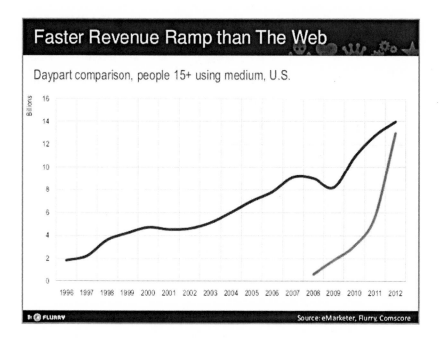

The term hockey stick is used in Silicon Valley to describe the revenue curve that moves from left to right in an upwards direction on the 'Revenue Projections' slide in the investment pitch deck. That's what VCs want to see. It's usually accompanied by the term 'exponential growth', which, after all, is the reason entrepreneurs need venture capital: to seize the opportunity at hand.

I have a feeling the next wave of entrepreneurs in the mobile and apps space will be replacing the words *hockey stick* with *near vertical*. By this, I'm talking about how steep the growth in mobile devices and apps have been compared to consumer internet adoption. Chatting to John Malloy, Co-Founder and General Partner of BlueRun Ventures, at a trade show in San Francisco last year, he made an excellent point that smart device adoption is ten times faster than the personal computer revolution, twice as fast as the internet boom and three times faster than the Facebook phenomenon.

It wasn't until I saw a slide deck from Simon Khalaf, CEO of Flurry, that I realized that mobiles had really changed the game and it was time to forget the hockey stick (blue line) and focus on the near vertical (green line)!

It's incredible that more people in the USA 15 years and older are spending time on mobile apps and the web (197 minutes per day) than on television (168 minutes) as of December 2012.

I'm an analyst by training. My first company, APT Strategies, provided online log file analysis and online surveys market intelligence to hundreds of websites in the 1990s. We partnered and eventually sold out to Jupiter Research Inc., which went to IPO in 1999. Poring over endless online analytics, data and forecasts in the roaring 1990s taught me to be somewhat statistically literate, so I take more than a casual glance at charts and numbers when I see them. I always look for a trend, triangulate it with a current event and draw a conclusion.

Apart from the hike in growth that fueled Facebook to sign up over 900 million users globally, there has never been such dramatic growth in usage of devices and technology than in the smartphone/tablet sector. It's just phenomenal growth.

The game has changed again, but this time mobile and apps took just a few short years to change it! Scary!

2

THE PITCH

Pitch Deck Essentials

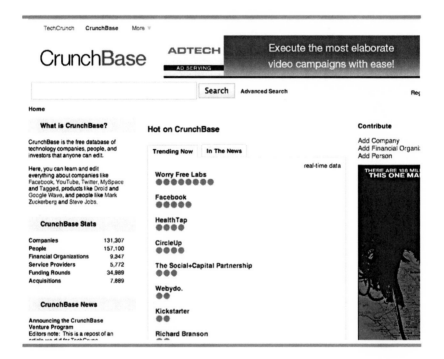

The most common question I am asked in Silicon Valley is, 'Can you help review my pitch deck?' A *pitch deck* is Silicon Valley speak for an investment presentation. Most entrepreneurs need help to craft their story. Most first-time entrepreneurs raising venture capital are not aware that there is a standard framework of slides that make up a typical investment presentation that Silicon Valley VCs like to see.

The first piece of advice I give to start-up founders is to keep it short and work to the model that VCs expect. The deck should be around 14 slides as follows:

Slide 1: Logo / Mission / Positioning Line. Founder Name(s).

Slide 2: Management Biographies

Slide 3: The Problem We Solve

Slide 4: The Solution

Slide 5: Market Size

Slide 6: Product / Technology Architecture / How It Works
(including product demo)

Slide 7: Scalability

Slide 8: Intellectual Property

Slide 9: Go to Market / Distribution Plan

Slide 10: Competition

Slide 11: Revenue Projections

Slide 12: Advisors

Slide 13: Use of Funds

Slide 14: Exit

It looks so simple doesn't it? I wish it was.

I first saw PayPal's pitch deck in the late 1990s and it was the simplest deck I'd ever seen. It was their Series C deck for $110 million.

Some advice for capital raising rookies: the simpler, the better. Shorten the number of words that come out of your mouth. The more that come out, the less ability the VC has to determine how exciting your company can be. You have to leave something to the imagination.

Most entrepreneurs don't realize that the average Silicon Valley VC is truly a jaded walking robot. They hear or read ten to fifteen pitches a week. You have to make them immediately understand your space, so don't go into so much detail that it becomes overwhelming.

Keep it high level. By *high level*, I mean: keep it to four or five points per slide. Don't make the common mistake of trying to tell your whole life story and how you got to be. You have 30 minutes. A VC won't tell you he's thinking in 30-minute blocks. Be prepared during phone or face-to-face pitches for the VCs to give you 30 minutes, so keep the presentation to 20 minutes then ask if they have questions. If the VCs like it, they'll stay longer than 30 minutes. If not, they'll politely tell you they have a 'hard stop' at 10.30, which is their way to cut the hour-long meeting they have made time for.

For those of you who aren't American, you should spend some time becoming familiar with the clichés and vernacular of VCs. They speak and think in a different frequency. In 2005, I called into see Evan Thornley at his home in East Melbourne, Australia. Evan, the founder of LookSmart, was always the gentleman. We sat down and discussed Silicon Valley and I remember he used the term 'the right frequency' when describing how best to pitch to US VCs. I've never forgotten this great advice. By *frequency*, Evan wasn't talking about repetitiveness, but rather the tone of an investment pitch. It's acute and something that VCs look for. Over the past ten years, I've sat in hundreds of meetings with VCs and often thought about how the right frequency can win over an investor.

Perhaps the most important part of the pitch is what I call the *right confidence frequency* — that is, whether the guy pitching really believe what he or she is saying. Are they a little desperate or tired by the sound of their own voice? Or are they busting with energy to seize the big opportunity and create a company that can own the space? It's very subtle and usually buried inside one of their sentences, the twinkle in the eye and how they interact with their co-founder.

VCs will often sit in meetings and ask the technical founder if he or she agrees with the CEO or founder. They are looking for friction between the founders. The slightest hint of apprehension can sway the VC towards a no. I've seen VCs get excited about an entrepreneur's product, only to view how the start-up team reacts to one another.

If there are two founders, both should speak in the meeting. It's important to break up the dialogue, which adds to the theatre of the presentation and emphasizes to the VC that you are a team and both have the right stuff. It allows the VCs to hear both the founders talk and presents a united front.

VCs use techniques to rat you out. I do it. The one technique I like the most is looking at the 'Go to Market' slide and asking what percentage of sales are going to come via the channel (resellers/ distributors) versus direct. Then, in the financials, I can see how they are stacking up the revenues and the resources to achieve these sales. Many start-up guys haven't thought through the practicalities of distribution.

If you're new to Silicon Valley, not sure how to approach a VC and don't know anyone, here are a few tips that go above and beyond going to a pitch fest and throwing your business card at them as they get off the stage from speaking or are being hailed by business cards as they scoot to the nearest exit.

The best way to approach a VC is to make sure you have reviewed their own professional endeavors on their profile pages and also look to see if there are any synergies between your product and their portfolio products. You can email them directly, but be sure to take an each-way bet: tell the VC how your product/technology could work with one of their portfolio companies.

VCs will gladly introduce you to a portfolio company if it makes commercial sense. I'd made an introduction on behalf of an entrepreneur to Clint Chao, managing partner at Formative Venture, who is on the board of Mashery. Specifically, I'd had the entrepreneur do the research and confirm their mobile platform could complement Mashery. This makes the introduction much more relevant and robust. VCs will list their investments on both their website and on websites such as *crunchbase.com*

When is the best time to go see a VC? When you have the scale question sorted out, and that often means at least three months of trend data — customer traction, sales uplift, etc. Perhaps the most common reason for a VC not being able to commit to an investment is the lack of customer traction and sales momentum that a start-up company can show in quantitative terms.

Finally, be prepared to be on your best behavior and bring your table manners! For the past six years, we've eaten at Il Fornaio in Cowper Street, Palo Alto, most weeks, either for lunch with start-up entrepreneurs or breakfast with other VCs. There's more to hearing a great pitch when you're going to back start-up guys. I like to see how they talk to waiters, their table manners and how they conduct themselves in a public place — watch them when they are more comfortable than being in a sterile boardroom with silence.

Slide 3: 'The Problem We Solve'

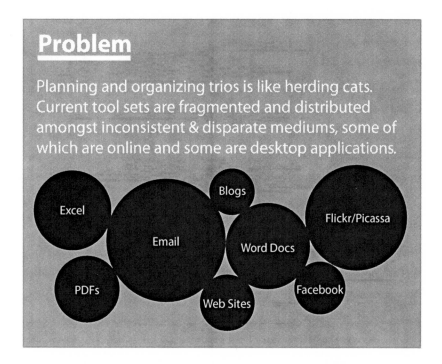

The first slide in the typical Silicon Valley investment pitch deck features the company name, logo and a one-line mission statement or positioning line. There is often another slide featuring the biographies and photos of the founders and management team.

The third slide is usually titled 'The Problem We Solve' or 'The Problem'. It is a concise statement explaining the problem that your start-up company is aiming to address.

My advice is to list the most important single problem you are trying to solve and not to complicate this slide with four or five bullet points. It is better to expand on the related or series of future problems verbally. You don't want to overwhelm the VCs with too many problems. Rather, focus on the problem that can be solved given the amount of money you are asking for in the capital raising and in the timeframe in which the money

being raised will last. VCs like to hear that the problem is *big* and fully understand there are many layers to it. They also like to see the problem broken down into stages that your technology can address in certain time frames.

Two of my friends, Chase Norlin and Alex Rowland, started a company called Alphabird Inc (*www.alphabird.com*) in 2009 in a basement office on Mission Street in San Francisco. I would drop in every few months and we would talk shop on video advertising networks and how finding niche video publishers of merit on YouTube was a huge problem for advertisers. I would offer advice and, being jazzed about their business, always make some introductions. In return, I became an advisory shareholder in their fledgling start-up.

Alphabird solves a big problem in helping to identify the most relevant video publishers on YouTube for advertisers. Advertisers want to reach the 800 million unique users who visit YouTube each month but have no idea where to start looking among the four billion videos watched each month. *That*'s a big problem to solve. In 2011, Alphabird was named in the Top 100 Brilliant Companies by *Entrepreneur Magazine* (*www.entrepreneur.com/magazine/index. html*).

The next important component of the 'The Problem We Solve'

slide is to emphasize that the problem is a severe pain that needs urgent relief. VCs will ask themselves how big a pain the problem is causing customers, as this will predetermine the elasticity of demand that your technology has — that is, how responsive customers will be to buy it.

I have seen many entrepreneurs fall into the trap of building a technology solution because they can without actually solving a burning problem.

During your investment pitch, articulate the problem clearly. Where possible, describe the problem in a real-life scenario by giving examples that the VC can relate to. Ideally, you will describe how the VC or their family members, client, etc. may encounter the problem.

While writing this chapter I learnt that Biz Stone, co-founder of Twitter, had just funded a company called CheckMate (*www.checkmate.io*), which aims to solve the pain of checking in to hotels and provide more options such as room upgrades offers, etc. Now, that is simple explanation of a pain or problem that many frequent travelers have. By making travelers aware of room upgrade options before getting to the front desk, CheckMate's website clearly articulates — and addresses — the problem.

Now that you have 'set up' the investors to understand the problem, you need to 'deliver' on your promise in the fourth slide, which explains and shows your technology solution.

There are three ways that entrepreneurs typically produce the 'Solution' slide.

Firstly, a screen capture of the homepage of the website or application. This visual should be nicely designed and have the impact to impress and excite the VCs.

Since the iPhone and app revolution, a very slick user interface

(UI) design is now a given in Silicon Valley. It's not something to do later. It's important at the get-go because users are fickle and expect the website and/or app to have a very intuitive UI and user experience (UX). Thanks to design marketplaces like oDesk (*www.odesk.com*), Elance (*www.elance.com*) and 99 Designs (*www.99designs.com.au*), getting a good logo and compelling website is relatively cheap. You need only pay hundreds rather than thousands of dollars. VCs see many pitches each week and are often fatigued by bland and lifeless presentations. The more visual the 'Solution' slide, the stronger the first impression and memory retention.

Secondly, entrepreneurs often present the 'Solution' slide by playing a 60-second video of the product. I really like this approach. A well-scripted video showing how the technology software works — explaining the functionality, interactivity, features and benefits with a voice over and background music — is an excellent way to communicate the solution. I've seen this done on many occasions and the one-minute video can really engage and enthuse the VCs.

Part of this video demonstration approach is pure theatre. It's designed to emotionally grab the investors and inspire them to believe in your start-up's mission by revealing the technology. Well-chosen screen captures, a professionally scripted voice over and video production can cost less than $500. I know, I have advised start-up technology companies to do this and they have been funded. There are amazingly talented professionals listed on oDesk and Elance who can produce these videos for you if you create the screen captures and script. They are TV production freelancers, semi-professional videographers and even web developers that are skilled in online video production.

In July 2012, I attended the Google Private Client Summit at the Fairmont Hotel in Chicago. Margo Georgiadis, President of the

Americas for Google, showed a video produced by Dollar Shave Club (*www.dollarshaveclub.com*). Take a moment now and view the video (*www.youtube.com/ZUG9qYTJMsI*). The 600-strong invitees knew this video was brilliant and flawlessly executed.

Imagine if you showed this type of video to VCs!

Now you've watched the video, you'll realize why it has gained over nine million video views and increased e-commerce revenue. It is a major reason they raised $9.8 million in a Series A venture capital round from Venrock Partners, Kleiner Perkins Caufield & Byers, Forerunner Ventures, Andreessen Horowitz, Shasta Ventures, and Felicis Ventures.

Now you can also understand why, with videos like this, it is a very unwise move to show VCs a series of mock-ups of the software unless it is actually coded and ready. If your technology solution is pre-alpha and at conceptual stage, I would suggest speaking to *friends and family* about investment, not VCs.

Thirdly, if your technology is a hardware product, it is critical to have a working prototype and show it working. Drawings may suffice, yet there is nothing like a real product to touch and demonstrate. If they technology is software, the VC may ask to see it working and you should be prepared to show them how the software works now or wait until the sixth slide, when you discuss the technology architecture and how it works.

Slide 5: 'Market Size'

U.S. Market

❖ **Over 4M US births each year**

❖ **Parent spending on education and childcare between $7K–$20K per child per year[2]**

The Parent University market includes families with children ages birth – 12

13 age groups X 4M / age group = 52M

52M X $120/user/year = $6.24B

Parent University Targeted US Market = $6.24 billion

The fifth slide the Silicon Valley VCs like to see is 'Market Size'. Now that the prospective investors have an understanding of the problem and how your technology solution solves this problem, it is important to quantify how big the potential market for your solution is. There are two key components to the 'Market Size' slide:

1. Total Available Market
2. Addressable Market

Quite often, entrepreneurs are not able to calculate how big the total addressable market is. Intel, for instance, launched in 1968 and to this day are creating new products and new markets. Did Google ever expect to acquire Motorola, a mobile phone company or be offering internet-enabled glasses? So VCs are aware that the total available market may be too large for you to accurately quantify. This is where the term *Disruptive Technology* most accurately describes the market size: disrupting a market to the point where new, uncontested markets open up is what W. Chan Kim and Renée Mauborgne's book *Blue Ocean Strategy* (Harvard Business School Press, 2005) explores. It's recommended reading for entrepreneurs.

The addressable market is a subset of the total available market and is typically a calculation of the piece of the total market your start-up is planning to target. Recently, I saw Chris Drew, CEO of Parent University, pitch his investment deck at a NestGSV (*www.nestgsv.com*) event in Redwood City. Chris stated the total available market for his mobile app was $70 billion, the total figure spent on kindergarten to year 12 education in the USA, yet the addressable market was $6.24 billion — the amount of money spent on children in the 0–6 age bracket. Chris also quoted both the US Department of Education and the Department of Labor, which is the correct way to underscore the validity of the information source. This is an example of a very clear explanation of the addressable market and the correct approach to present the Market Size slide.

If you can't articulate or quantify the market size, it can be difficult for VCs to qualify the opportunity. It's important to provide a definitive picture of the available and addressable markets as best you can.

Slide 6: 'Product / Technology Architecture / How It Works'

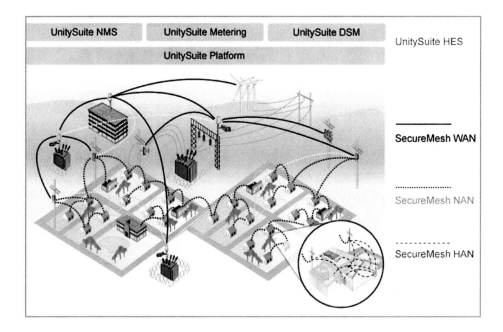

Although you have previously introduced the product in the 'Solution' slide by either showing the website, the hardware or, in most cases, the software platform or application, further explanation is now needed.

This slide gives an overview of the product / technology architecture and how it works. I always recommend building this product / technology architecture slide in order to clearly show how a user or customer would engage with the technology and how the technology stack or architecture fits together. It is important to diagrammatically map out the physical hardware and software components and how they interrelate and/or are connected.

This may require illustrating how microprocessors, CPU, middleware components, servers, databases, computers, mobile phones and internet all fit together. It is often a challenge to illustrate your processes on one PowerPoint slide; however, it is a crucial task that helps you present your technology business to the VCs using pictures, icons, drawings or graphical designs. For many VCs, seeing how your technology interacts with customers allows then to grasp it visually.

As you are discussing the technology architecture, if your technology is software and demonstrable, now is the perfect segueway to demonstrate the software working. Don't presume that the VCs already have an intricate knowledge of your hardware or software. Acronyms should not be part of the presentation unless they are very well known. By the same token, obscure or highly technical acronyms can cause VCs to second-guess and may even lead to misinterpretation. Where possible, create a real-life scenario that a VC can easily understand.

I always encourage entrepreneurs to speak in the first person when explaining the technology architecture slide. That is, speak as if you are the user and explain the process (e.g. 'When I click this button …').

Be sure to speak about the defensibility of the product and technology at this point as well. It may be that there is a uniqueness in the design or process. VCs want the product / architecture slide to demonstrate that there is a point of difference and originality, and clearly defined intellectual property. They will be focused on how your technology works differently from any competitors, so be sure to explain it and give insights into the 'secret sauce'. This is important, as you don't want to let VCs assume that there isn't a point of product differentiation. Be sure to discuss how your product is designed to win customers more easily or solve the challenges that competitor products are not equipped to face.

The seventh slide of a typical investment deck shown to Silicon Valley VCs focuses on scalability, intellectual property and defensibility.

The private dining room at Il Fornaio restaurant on Cowper Street in Palo Alto is an unlikely place for a meeting with a start-up I was advising and assisting with angel investor introductions. Shaking off the rain from my umbrella, I shuffled through the crowded Friday lunchtime, making my way to the back of the restaurant. I was greeted by Nick Evans, cofounder of TILE, a start-up that built a hardware/

firmware device that can be attached to objects and used to find them via a mobile phone app. The long dining table that could comfortably sit 20 people was set for a culinary feast. As Nick greeted me with a firm handshake I was expecting more people in the room, but it was empty with only an Apple MacBook laptop connected to an iPad mini on the table.

'Who needs an office when you have this?' beamed Nick, referring to the spacious room he'd got for free for an hour from his restaurant hostess friend. That's a good sign: a scrappy entrepreneur using empty dining rooms at downtown Palo Alto restaurants. Nice work, I thought to myself.

Nick took me through the deck with his partner Mike beaming in on FaceTime via the iPad mini, chiming in as we moved through the slides. It was the first time I'd seen the investment deck and I could almost hear the mental gears grinding inside the heads of these two hardcore engineers as they stumbled through the 'dry run' presentation. I always suggest that entrepreneurs pitch to advisors with their investment deck to practice, get feedback and, most of all, to project their business verbally. This crystalizes the obvious areas that need improvement and helps founders make hard decisions on priorities.

The last thing you want to do is have investors feel you are ambivalent on a go-to-market strategy or undecided whether your software is a consumer-facing product or an integration play. That suggests increased chances of a 'pivot', which to a VC means a big risk.

Utilize advisors to chisel your investment presentation and help you prioritize which story you want to tell in your investment pitch. While you honestly may not know how your technology will be received by a segment, whether you need to change business models or tweak the product, you have to show the investor that you are steadfast in terms of the company direction and also that you can back yourself in executing your ideas. The investor wants to see conviction.

The slide deck was looking better than the first two versions now that it included the critical slide on scalability. Perhaps one of the most frequently asked questions I hear from investors here in Silicon Valley is, 'How does this scale?' and in many ways it's the hardest question to answer. Not all software companies have a viral component, which is the simplest form of scale as it involves word of mouth and referrals by friends to others. Think: eBay, Facebook, PayPal.

TILE had now baked scalability into their model. The app downloaded onto mobile phones would act as detection device. If, say, a pet was lost and wandered into a neighbor's yard, the TILE would signal the app, which would notify the owner. This is scale, as the app would be referred to friends by friends or communities of pet lovers. Not only was TILE smaller, with a longer battery life than other mobile detection devices, but its price point was also being pitched was $10. Now that's cheap enough for impulse purchases and, more importantly, to be distributed rapidly as promotional items or giveaways funded by merchants.

This exponential model is what VCs want to see in an investment deck. Virality and word of mouth create very powerful companies that grow without large marketing budgets. VCs love quick-growing adoption curves.

As I stared at the iPad mini and played with the TILE app on my iPhone 5, I realized that these two devices were the first Apple products released after Steve Jobs's death in October 2011. Things were getting smaller than ever. That was part of the appeal of Apple products: they were slimmer, smaller and boutique.

Scalable businesses that grow faster than what traditional financing attracts, such as business overdrafts, is what venture capital is for. If VCs feel the scale question isn't answered, they typically refrain from investing in a company.

After helping TILE further with their investment deck, they were ready to start speaking with investors. In January 2013, I introduced the founders of TILE to Doug Renert, who runs Tandem (*www. tandemcap.com*), a Silicon Valley–based accelerator focused on mobile start-ups. The following month, TILE was accepted into Tandem's accelerator program and received an initial $200,000 investment.

Slide 8: 'Intellectual Property'

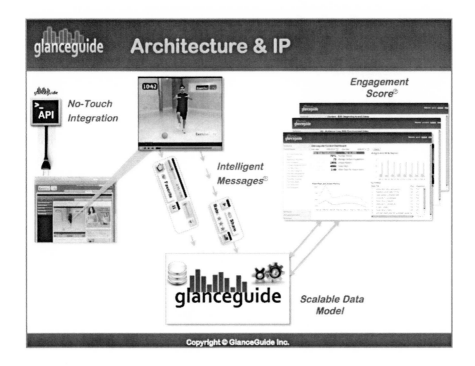

Intellectual Property (IP) is a term that most entrepreneurs are familiar with yet don't necessarily fully understand. Entrepreneurs need to explain the IP in their technology when pitching. This slide can form part of Slide 7 but can also be a separate slide in the investment deck.

The most common first step mistake for entrepreneurs in Silicon Valley is to put 'patent pending technology' in their investment deck. This is usually dismissed by VCs, as it more often than not evidences the founders have filed a provisional patent with the US Patent and Trademark Office (*www.uspto.gov*). Too often I hear founders say, 'We've filed a provisional patent.' Heads up, my friends: this is *not* substantial enough to impress VCs. What you're really saying is, I spent a few hundred bucks and got a one-year option to file a legitimate patent.

Entrepreneurs, the smarter approach is to explain in your investment pitch that you have an IP strategy. State in the investment pitch that your IP protection will ensure defensibility of your technology against competitors. That's a good start.

I've counseled many entrepreneurs on how to answer the common VC question, 'Can you tell me a little more about your IP?' I've also been fortunate to spend time with patent attorneys. Good IP attorneys, like my friend Richard Horton, who has worked at top law firms such as DLA Piper and Squire Sanders, have mapped out some brilliant patent licensing and technology licensing strategies for technology companies, and my advice to entrepreneurs is to spend time with patent attorneys and seek their counsel. As an entrepreneur, you will benefit from getting to know attorneys in your field. Reach out to them and introduce yourself. Buy them lunch. Talk to them. Charm them. They always need expert domain opinions and access to intelligent people like yourself.

If that isn't a feasible option, without getting too specific, you can search on *www.uspto.gov* for patents that already exist in your field, which helps determine if a patent has already been granted. You definitely need to understand what has been patented in your field and ensure there are no similar patents that could result in a future patent infringement case.

In 2009, my friend and fellow San Jose Sharks ice hockey fan, Yar Chaikovsky, who practices as an Intellectual Property Litigation Attorney at McDermott Will & Emery in Menlo Park, California, called me to review some patents based on search engine submissions technology. I was happy to help. What you learn when you review patents is that there are lots of people who have vision beyond their years and can patent processes that are not even in existence at the time they write the patents.

So think hard about your IP strategy, spend some time online reviewing which patents are already filed, and create products that are unique to avoid being sued for infringement if and when your product becomes popular.

IP is an intriguing field. I'm particularly interested in how technology impacts brands and how to protect brands from trademark and service mark infringements. In 2011, I, together with my business partners Tyron Ball, co-founder/CEO of WebIP (*www.webip.com.au*), began designing and building a new brand management platform to help ensure that intellectual web property is managed for large brands. Today, WebIP technology platform allows big brands like News Corporation, Mercedes Benz, Fuji Xerox, Toshiba and Virgin to monitor the impact that social media, video, blogs and forums have on their domain names, brand names and trademarks.

Show your VCs that you have an IP strategy, not just a patent idea or filing. Showing VCs that you understand the importance and relevance of intellectual property will help in your capital-raising experience. Including IP and patent filings into your technology product roadmap is a critical part of the future success of your company.

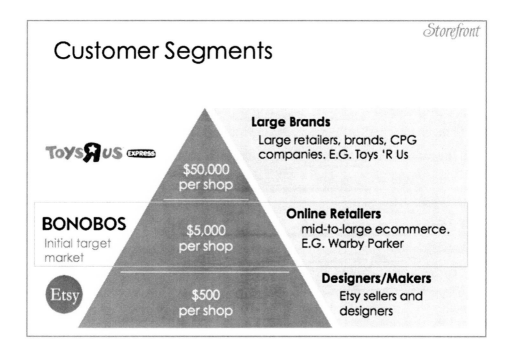

The 'Go to Market' slide speaks about segments such as consumers, medium businesses or retailers. However, I encourage entrepreneurs to dig deeper into this slide and articulate exactly who they are selling to.

VCs may not ask who the customer is at a job description level but they will certainly think about it as you are presenting. VCs, unlike some entrepreneurs pitching for angel or seed investment, often conjure up the image of the founders sitting in front of a customer and then ask themselves, 'Who is this person?' Is it the marketing director, logistics manager or chief financial officer?

VCs say no to lots of investments because the actual person being sold to is mismatched with the offering. For instance, in recent times, I've listened to many mobile app start-up investment pitches and, on several occasions, they don't know who in the organization they will sell to. Is it the sales directors or the IT managers? If you're selling to developers, these people are often hobbyists and often don't buy products. They roll between free trials to get tools for free. The point is that you need to think through who is the ultimate buyer and be explicit to VCs about their propensity to purchase.

If the product is sold to enterprise customers, there are typically longer sales cycles than consumer products. You need to be aware of the risk-averse investor looking at long sales cycles requiring greater amounts of venture capital.

I see VCs asking to speak to prospective or existing customers of start-ups as part of their due diligence. Entrepreneurs should always speak about their customers' buying patterns and decision-making cycles when talking to investors.

SLIDE 9: 'GO TO MARKET'

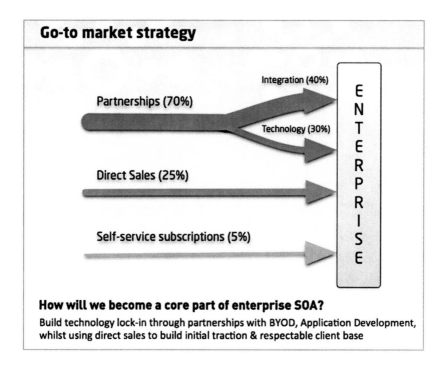

The ninth slide of a typical investment deck focuses on your 'Go to Market' plan — in other words, how your product will enter the market, which segments your product will be distributed to, and how these distribution channels will lead to fast growth and scale.

Once, I was conducting some due diligence on a start-up based in San Francisco. So I rang a friend, Jerry Inguagiato, to ask him about what he thought of a new commercial real estate online marketplace called StoreFront, based up in San Francisco. Jerry is Senior Vice President of CBRE, the world's premier, full-service real estate services company, which is based in San Jose, California. San Jose is home to Adobe, eBay and other large tech start-ups and is the 'South Bay' of the Bay Area, as the locals call it.

The thing about VCs in Silicon Valley is that their network affords them the opportunity to ask at a high level if a new start-up would disrupt, replace or be well received by incumbent players or channel players in a market. That's what Jerry and I were discussing on the phone.

Nothing can ruin a start-up funded company quicker than a channel that won't assist in the distribution of a new product, doesn't see an opportunity for the start-up technology to save them time and/ or make them money. This is the secret to the channel positioning of a start-up. Tell the VC that you've spoken to channel partners and, if possible, have one join your advisor board. Ask the channel partner for a Letter of Intent, a distribution reseller agreement or a testimonial. Do anything to get the commitment from them that validates your business model in the eyes of the VC. If you don't, the VC will ring one of their friends at the golf club who is an attorney who represents a competitor, a country club pal who they see at the gym after work, a school parent they bump into at Peet's Coffee in the morning, their neighbor who is retired or wife's friends husband that works at Intuit. Make no mistake, this happens so fast and frequently.

Remember: the VC will call customers, clients, channel partners and anyone else in an effort to turn over every stone to validate your 'Go to Market' strategy and make sure your start-up has a viable distribution channel that will embrace your product technology and not thwart it.

I received an email from StoreFront founder and CEO Erik Eliason shortly after I had introduced him to Jerry from CBRE, saying, 'Yes, Jerry at CBRE has been great. He introduced us to his partners in LA and we will have retail space across the street from Disneyland. This will be a great space to enter the LA market.' By properly undertaking the due diligence of the start-up's channel market, I was able to make an introduction to CBRE, which resulted in a business opportunity for StoreFront. This illustrates how VCs can help start-up founders advance their 'Go to Market' while at the same time conducting due diligence.

Competitors — WebIP.

	WebIP	MELBOURNE IT	CitizenHawk	MarkMonitor	Go Daddy	network solutions	NetNames
Domain Renewals	Y	Y	Y	Y	Y	Y	Y
Domain Registration	Y	Y	Y	Y	Y	Y	Y
List 3rd Party Domain	Y	✗	✗	✗	✗	✗	✗
Domain Monitoring	Y	✗	✗	✗	✗	✗	✗
Trademark Listing	Y	✗	✗	Y	✗	✗	✗
Trademark Monitoring	Y	✗	✗	✗	✗	✗	✗
Trademark Search	Y	✗	✗	✗	✗	✗	✗
Brand Monitoring	Y	✗	✗	✗	✗	✗	✗
Case Management	Y	Y	Y	Y	✗	✗	Y
Contract Management	Y	✗	✗	✗	✗	✗	✗
Multi Users	Y	Y	Y	Y	✗	Y	Y
Permission Restrictions	Y	Y	Y	Y	✗	✗	Y

Although the 'Competition' slide is tenth in the deck, it is the first slide that I recommend entrepreneurs put together. This is because it is something that needs to be considered carefully before embarking on an enterprise.

A matrix showing competitors and their attributes, features and price points is the best format for presenting the 'Competition' slide and is well understood by investors. It shows that you've thought about the competitors and provides the opportunity to speak to specific areas of strength and differentiation over them.

As much as VCs like to see uniqueness in product, they understand competitors validate a market and raise the noise level. Some VCs believe that all boats rise with the tide, meaning all competitors do well in an emerging sector due to competition.

If you don't include this slide, VCs will discover the competitors pretty easily for themselves using Google. Don't think that your investment deck is definitive. VCs are doing their own research as you're talking!

Slide 11: 'Revenue Projections/ Business Model'

4 year financials

	Y1	Y2	Y3	Y4
Revenues				
Direct Enterprise Customers	490,000	1,050,000	1,300,000	4,100,000
Integration/Channel partners	110,000	1,500,000	3,500,000	6,200,000
Self-service subscriptions	35,0000	90,000	150,000	300,000
Total	**635,000**	**2,140,000**	**4,950,000**	**10,600,000**
Operating Expenses				
CEO	100,000	110,000	120,000	130,000
Engineering	310,000	680,000	920,000	1,335,000
Sales & BD	285,000	390,000	780,000	1,300,000
Marketing	65,000	130,000	205,000	345,000
Customer Support	60,000	100,000	140,000	200,000
Admin & Incidentals	30,000	75,000	100,000	200,000
Corporate rental	50,000	50,000	80,000	120,000
Total	**900,000**	**1,535,000**	**2,345,000**	**3,630,000**
EBITDA	**-265,000**	**605,000**	**2,605,000**	**6,970,000**
Head count	**7**	**17**	**24**	**39**

Hitting your numbers, the Silicon Valley term for achieving your revenue projections, is often the slide that entrepreneurs struggle with the most. Slide 11, which forecasts the revenue for one to five years, is the slide the VC wants to see to understand how the entrepreneur has modeled the financial projections.

Before drilling down into the financial revenue projections, the business model should be explained. The business model is how the company makes money. If the business model is uncertain, I suggest entrepreneurs not whole heartedly commit to the financial projections and emphasize they are subject to change - which investors understand. Once commercial contracts have been signed with customers you avoid the risk of pre-determining a business model that doesn't eventuate.

If your company is at the *friends and family* stage and not ready for seed funding, I would favor leaving the revenue projections slide out of the investment deck. If you are raising seed capital, it must be included.

My advice is not to put in a pricing plan for your product or service based on a progressive scale or a *freemium* (free for some features, paid for others) model without specifically providing a 'Profit and Loss' summary on Slide 11 of the investment deck.

The 'Revenue Projections' slide should have the following for years one to five:

projected sales
    less: cost of goods sold (if applicable)
    less: labor and development costs
    less: general and admin costs
    less: marketing and customer acquisition costs
    equals = earnings before tax
    net cash flow position (sales less earnings before tax)
    head count (i.e. number of employees)

It's pretty simple. VCs know the numbers move around as the business progresses, but they are looking for clarity of mind and a financial model from entrepreneurs. Don't pluck numbers out of the air or run a macro spreadsheet with incremental percentage formulas to calculate future-year revenue and expenses. It is a rookie error to drag formula cells from one row to another in an Excel spreadsheet to produce five-year forecasts.

I remember being in several meetings with Richard Ling, Managing Partner at Rembrandt Ventures on Sand Hill Road. Richard would actually move his lips as he was doing the mental arithmetic to calculate the growth of revenue he was reviewing and whether it had a potential exit high enough to warrant a venture capital investment. Not all VCs give you the benefit of their body language but, rest assured, they are calculating percentage increases over each year as you're talking through your 'Revenue Projections' slide.

As you'll be asked every month post-funding to prepare updated financials and forecasts, it's important you *get behind the numbers* — a term used by VCs in the Valley to describe understanding the financial assumptions that are used in preparing the financial forecasts. You must give some context to the financial assumptions and don't assume that the investors will believe nominal numbers.

Be it subscribers multiplied by a monthly charge, a percentage of sales or a function of customer growth rates and or license fee revenue, it is extremely important to show the VC that you are financially literate. You don't have to get complicated; no one expects a complex financial model. Keep it is easy to compute, and remember that part of the art of raising venture capital is being able to explain simply how you will 'hit your numbers'.

Savvy investors will pick up on the slightest eye movement, denoting your hesitation or showing uncertainty, when it comes to this slide. They watch for it. You need to speak clearly and concisely and create a very simple math equation for them. A good entrepreneur will say that one customer can blow out the revenue projections. That excites the VC. Telling them that you are tracking above a certain metric that is important to bringing in revenue is also compelling. This may be engagement or usage frequency metrics.

Whatever you do, don't hesitate when speaking about the revenue model. You must be able to explain it. If you can't, don't pitch it. Work out an easy-to-understand financial model. Don't get into sensitivity analysis based on pricing. It's too complex. If you have resellers or distributors, put a percentage of revenue against this channel per year. Don't lump all the revenue into one line if you have different revenue streams. That said, keep it to two or three revenue lines; otherwise, there is too much detail on the slide.

Although a VC may pass on the current investment round, they often record the financial projections and ask the entrepreneur for an update in six or 12 months to see if the revenue projections given were met. I always recommend that entrepreneurs update these VCs on a six-monthly basis regarding revenue figures. That's a great way to ensure that you are invited back to pitch for later rounds of capital being raised.

Slide 12: 'Advisors'

Investors & Advisors

David Tisch
Founder, TechStars NYC

Thomas Korte
Founder, AngelPad

Robert Stephens
Founder, GeekSquad

Katherine Barr
General Partner, MDV

Yulie Kim
VP Product, One Kings Lane

Shelby Clark
Founder, RelayRides

I don't really have a sweet tooth yet find myself frequenting Sprinkles, the cupcake store at Stanford Mall (*www.sprinkles.com*) in Palo Alto, with Cassie, my youngest daughter at least fortnightly. Being a keen observer of human behavior, I have noticed that people tend to ask the store assistants more questions about the cupcakes with sprinkles than the plain cupcakes with cream on top. One day, I was sitting in Sprinkles looking over two investment pitch decks when it dawned on me: If investment decks were cupcakes, advisors are sprinkles — you tend to look at the cupcakes with sprinkles first!

Including the name of advisors on a slide is not just for appearances. Advisors help shape the company, provide valuable insights for the founders on product strategy, go-to-market contacts, technical aspects and competitor activity. An advisor slide in the deck, featuring a headshots and two-line bio for each advisor, show investors that reputable people have validated you and your idea and are willing to help grow the company.

In Silicon Valley, most start-ups have between three and six advisors. The advisors' current executive position also helps investors think through potential partnerships and sales channels that your start-up may have. It's eye candy at the very least and evidence of the your personal network at best.

Being an entrepreneur can be a lonely road and it helps to have advisors who can make the journey more productive and enjoyable. I've always formed advisor boards in my tech start-ups and strongly encourage entrepreneurs to do the same.

Advisors typically don't invest any money in the start-up company and in exchange for lending their profile on the investment deck or website and providing some advice, they receive a small piece of the entrepreneurs' stock. In Silicon Valley, the going rate for an advisor is typically 0.25–1 percent of the common founders' stock; this is the normal equity given to an advisor for 12 to 18 months in a pre-seed round company — though I have seen cases where it has gone as low as 0.10 percent. I typically like to see advisor agreements struck in the early part of the company formation for at least one to two years and then more advisors joining by issuing stock options once the company is funded beyond the seed round of capital.

Choosing advisors that provide a holistic viewpoint is important. Don't surround yourself with people who say yes. Entrepreneurs need to be challenged. I always suggest that the entrepreneur draw a circle on a piece of paper and then slices it into pizza pieces. Write on each pizza slice the type of skills the start-up company needs to complement the team's core competencies.

Choose people who have expertise in a particular field and, importantly, who you actually like. This inner circle of advisors should have a personal relationship with you, so you can also reach out to them personally. The larger investors will typically take board seats and, in my experience, are not often personally invested in the entrepreneur. They want a return on their money; the relationship is purely commercial. They often don't want to know what goes on or get involved in your personal life.

Start-ups are emotional rollercoasters, and having a friend in the passenger seat that you can vent to, let off steam with, have a coffee or beer with and talk openly with is really important. Make it clear to them that this is a venture that may succeed, but may not! Advisors should be advisors because they like you, regardless of how the company performs. If your start-up fails, an advisor should still be your friend.

Having acted on dozens of start-up advisory boards, I still often see entrepreneurs and investors involved in start-ups that didn't work. Without exception, we remain on very good terms — regardless of whether there was an exit or not. Be sure to think about an advisor's reaction to you and your friendship should your start-up not work out. That's the true test of whether the advisor is worthy of being included in the slide deck.

SLIDE 13: 'USE OF FUNDS'

Current Raise

Seed Round of $750k @ $2.8M valuation

Use of proceeds:

- **Focus on direct enterprise sales initially to build immediate revenue - Hire a business development & sales guy**
- **Build channel & Integration Partnership program**
- **Deploy to 25 new enterprise customers by June 2012 (~500k sales)**
- **Build community, documentation, improve core product features**

Typically, the 'Use of Funds' slide is divided into the following sections:

- Staff/Labor Costs
- General and Operational Expenses
- Technology/Capital Expenses.

It is a very useful slide in the investment pitch deck, as it forces you to think about how you will spend the venture capital. It also enables you to focus on exactly how much money is needed to reach your objectives and avoid the mistake of raising too much capital. This slide is an opportunity for entrepreneurs to demonstrate financial discipline.

Let me explain.

Anyone in the Valley will tell you that raising venture capital can be an unfair game. That's because there are no rules on how much you should and can raise. Ninety-nine percent of start-ups don't get funded, which makes it absurd when you stumble across a company that has raised too much money.

Once, a Los Altos–based entrepreneur raised $750,000 in seed capital at a pre-money valuation of $3 million. This amount was not unreasonable, given he had a great team with a successful track record. He then raised another $1 million and, when I met him, he was looking for another $250,000 to *top up the round* — which, in Silicon Valley terms, suggests a ceiling figure for a venture raising. This was an e-commerce technology start-up that had not produced any revenue and employed three full-time sales executives and three technical developers. I told him point blank that, with a post-money valuation of $6 million with zero customers and zero revenue, he could be in a lot of trouble in the next capital-raising round. He didn't hit the $1.5 million revenue figure forecasted for the first 12 months and faced a serious problem of a reduced valuation which very had a very negative impact on employees, all of whom are working to get rich from their stock options packages. The bottomline impact when too much money is raised and revenue targets aren't met is that valuations in future rounds are often less significant and this causes shareholder dissatisfaction.

I understand the argument for loading up a huge round of money to go after a global market, which is what Square did with their $100 million Series C and $200 Million Series D (see *www.crunchbase.com/company/square*) and what Airbnb did with their $112 million

Series B (see *www.crunchbase.com/company/airbnb*) but these are later-stage rounds, not the first round where the product is being built and sales are yet to come.

Raising too much money is a trap for rookies, and those with egos seem to need the stroking without thinking of the consequences. It is a dangerous game that inexperienced entrepreneurs get sucked into. The golden rule in my book is: in your first round of funding, only raise enough money to hit your milestones, be that product development or proving out sales. Seed rounds should have capital deployed over six to nine months, and Series A should be 12 to 24 months. Don't raise too much too soon, or you risk overshooting your runway of matching product with revenue and end up in a precarious situation where your company valuation is compromised for the next venture capital round.

Having a very detailed use of funds slide in the investment pitch deck ensures that you are communicating to investors that the entrepreneur has thought through how they will spend the money. I encourage entrepreneurs to work through this "cost up" approach to identify where money will be spent which in turn calculates the amount of funds required. This exercise will remove the risk in raising too much capital which can lead to unnecessary expenditure and ultimately diminish the risk of a lower valuation on future rounds of raising capital.

Slide 14: 'Exit'

The 'Exit' slide is typically the last in the investment pitch deck. It should feature companies from three or four different sectors or industries. The aim here is to show investors that there is diversity among potential acquirers.

My advice is to put nice big icons and logos of companies that are potential acquirers. Put in a Cisco logo, a Juniper Networks logo, an American Express Logo or Walmart logo.

Investors are typically older than start-up founders and, by virtue of their age, know a few more people. As part of the due diligence process, it is common for them to call up a buddy or associate at the firms you put into your 'Exit' slide and ask if they are looking at this space, made any investments, using any competitor products, etc. This is a typical part of the investors' due diligence and important for entrepreneurs to know.

Do your homework on the investors you are pitching. If it makes sense, include in the 'Exit' slide some companies that the VC you are pitching to has been involved with, or their firm has been involved with. This is a simple but smart, tactical move that allows you to leverage the meeting with those investors who say no but are keen to introduce you to someone they know at those companies. It's a good idea to always ask the VCs if they can introduce you to someone at one of these companies or at least someone who used to work there. It's considered a given by venture capitalists in Silicon Valley to make introductions to your network when a start-up entrepreneur asks. It shows good faith and fosters the ecosytem of innovation. Venture capitalists make introductions on behalf of entrepereneurs so they can build up their reputation as a helpful person which is a way to garner business leads.

Entrepreneurs should think about this when crafting their Exit slide as the companies on the Exit slide are usually vastly different from those who eventually make the acquisition.

Determining a Valuation

Valuation is one of the more varying and possibly the most complex part of the capital-raising process. Technically, the precise valuation of the company varies throughout the raising of capital.

Friends and Family

The first phase of raising money for your start-up is *friends and family*, which is exactly that. It's where, without much more than an idea or the product in concept stage, trusted people that have known you for a very long time invest in your personal equity. That is, they know you are a person of ability and intelligence and hope that writing a *blind check* (a Silicon Valley term for money invested in good faith without seeing the product) will result in a return.

My advice is to give up ten percent of your start-up company in a *family and friends* round. It does not really matter what the valuation is because typically you are using the money to pay your expenses to build the product. If it is $75,000, then the pre-money valuation of your company is $675,000 and the post-money valuation is $750,000 (pre-money valuation + $75,000). In this scenario, you're offering ten percent of the equity as consideration for the $75,000.

Investors wanting to support your idea often think that you need enough money to pay the equivalent of wages if you were working in a full-time job outside of your own start-up. This is a sensible way to look at a *friends and family* round as it is a simple way to explain to investors the amount entrepreneurs should raise.

Jason Calacanis (angel investor and organizer of the Launch Conference — see *blog.launch.co*) best described how it should feel as an investor who writes the first check into a company. We were talking after he spoke at one of Adeo Ressi's Founders Institute (*fi.co/*) events at the Microsoft Campus in Mountain View in the Valley in 2010. Jason was spot on when he said, 'If I'm going to write a $100,000 check, I want to feel that I'm getting at least ten percent because I'm in their first check and want a chunk of the company that is meaningful.'

Jason made a very good point about how family and friends *feel* about writing that blind check. They want a sizable piece of equity that *feels good* for their trust in the entrepreneur. And that's fair enough! Entrepreneurs should understand that they often need to think past the actual dollar size and recognize that there is emotion in investing. Investors need to feel comfortable and that is often not a quantitative measurement!

Angel and Seed Capital

Seed capital typically ranges between $250,000 and $750,000 and should provide the *financial runway* (Silicon Valley speak for how long the money raised will last) for nine to 12 months. After the dot-com crash in 2000 up until 2006, start-up valuations at the seed round were most often exceeding $2.5 million pre-money on a $500,000 round. Convertible notes were virtually nonexistent as founders of start-up companies were happy just to get investors! It was a lean time for entrepreneurs in the Valley.

Fast-forward five years to 2013 and it's a whole different ballgame. We've seen a dramatic growth in angel investors, accelerator funds like Y Combinator and other angel investment vehicles pushing cash into start-ups using uncapped convertibles notes that convert at a 20 percent discount to the eventual Series A. From 2005 to 2013, Silicon Valley has seen an unprecedented level of investment in the angel and seed rounds.

From 2009 to 2012 (before Facebook had an initial public offering, or *IPO'd*), there was a dramatic rise in valuations for start-ups. During this period, I regularly advised entrepreneurs who had raised money on convertible notes at a pre-money of between $4 million and $7 million when they had zero revenue. I told many of them they had an *overcooked valuation* (a Silicon Valley term describing an excessive valuation, given the stage of the company). For many entrepreneurs looking to raise $500,000+ on pre-money of $4 million to $7 million in 2009 to 2012, I would encourage you to consider raising the seed round at between $2.5 million and $3 million pre-money. When a start-up has no revenue and still forming a team with product iterations, it's a dangerous time to value a company because it is so arbitrary — based only on the size of the opportunity, on the team to execute on building a product, and with unknown competitors who may not yet have emerged. I am always skeptical of any start-up who has raised small increments of money on increased valuations over a period when they can't demonstrate product engagement or customer traction.

Recently, Joe Kennedy — my partner in Arafura Ventures — and I met up with some entrepreneurs from the gaming industry at The Stanford Park Hotel on El Camino Real in Menlo Park. It's a great hotel for meetings, away from the crowded cafes in downtown Palo Alto. The four guys had left Zynga Inc. to start a new games company. They were raising between $600,000 and $750,000 on a post-money valuation of $8 million. Gee whizz, I thought to myself, that's $2 million dollars per founder. How good can they be when Zynga's (Nasdaq: ZNGA) share price had plummeted from $14 to $2.50 in 2012?

That's another way that VCs look at a start-up value. Divide the valuation of the company by the number of employees at the time of the raising. If they were applying for a job at their experience level, would their employment package and stock options equate to the amount they are asking per employee of their own start-up? Even if you added a 30 or 50 percent premium to include the risk involved, would that valuation be reasonable? Well, in this case it was not, and I think its an important calculation that entrepreneurs should make when determining their company valuation and discussing a seed investment with investors.

Series A and B, and Later Valuations

Valuations for Series A and B often vary widely and depend upon the trajectory of the company. There are no norms that apply, so I should explain that, upon an exit after a Series A and B round, the VCs would like to have the founders (assuming there are two or more founders) holding 15 to 20 percent each of the company. This means that, following a Seed, Series A and Series B, the founders have enough of a stake to ensures they make the most money, assuming all the investors are diversified.

In general, Series A investments are $3 million to $6 million on average, and Series B $6 million to $15 million on average. However, they vary a lot depending on the capital intensity of the company.

Series C, D and E are later-stage rounds of venture capital that are often raised before an exit via a trade sale or an IPO on the stock market. There are also other forms of finance typically taken on by venture-backed companies in later stages, including mezzanine financing such as debt and/or preferred equity.

3

AFTER THE PITCH

CLOSING INVESTORS

Like most salespeople, entrepreneurs have to close the deal with investors. So how do you know if a VC is interested? And how do you orchestrate closing the deal? These are questions I am often asked by start-up founders.

While there are various components to this, a critical part of the sales process for entrepreneurs is to know when VCs are showing signs of investing. Detecting 'buying signals' early is important and, after that, it's imperative that you capitalize on them.

Here are some tips.

Firstly, investors will give you what I call the *steel glare*. You have to look closely at the VCs and understand that, at some point, their eyes will glaze over or they'll become intense. Look close enough and their pupils will dilate when they see you as an object of interest. This is why, when acting in the capacity of a VC, I always sit with my back to the window, so that the light doesn't artificially constrict my pupils and also to ensure entrepreneurs aren't getting a false reading of my intent.

At some point in your investor presentations, you're going to get the prospective investor making some stern comments that may at first appear brash. Human emotion manifests itself in the investor in their being more tense than usual, being unemotional, almost as if they don't like you. I've noticed over my many years of being in investment pitches, either as an advisor to start-ups, aides to VC firms or as part of the venture team, that at some point the VC will make some comment to the entrepreneur that is harsh. It's like they are shifting gears. It might be something like, 'You better like working Sundays,' or 'You need to focus more on sales' or, 'I expect you to make us 15x on this investment.' These comments are normal as part of the VC's mental commitment to your business. I urge entrepreneurs not to take it personally. Read between the lines here and realize that VCs are not making a personal assault, but rather bolstering their position as an authority in the post-funding relationship they plan to have with you. Recognize that, when an investor speaks down to you in an investment meeting, they are actually committing to an investment in your company.

The tone of voice underlines their concern, as they are staking their reputation on the investment and are giving you the Al Pacino in *Scarface*-type speech not to screw them over. It's also a way for VCs to try and assert their superiority over you. Don't be intimidated by their bullying tactics (it's the banker in them). And remember: they, too, are scared, and this causes anxiety and nervousness. It doesn't matter how many wins a VC has had with start-ups. Failure is still a heartbeat away, and VCs often have more to lose than entrepreneurs have to gain in terms of reputation! VCs want to keep you in a position where you have a fear of them, to an extent, which helps keep you motivated to succeed.

In May 2011, I spoke at the *Biblio-Tech: Using a Humanities Ph.D. in Silicon Valley* conference at Stanford University, where Mike Moritz, legendary investor and Sequoia Capital partner, also spoke. If you've heard Mike speak, you'll know he doesn't suffer fools.

During the conference break, another speaker told me the story of how another Sequoia Partner, Pierre Lamond would grill YouTube co-founder Steve Chen and Steve was always on the edge of his seat at those monthly board meetings.

Entrepreneurs thinking about closing the round of venture capital, need to demonstrate some "chutzpah" and resolve so the venture capitalist doesn't intimidate or walk over them. A good venture capitalist will look for that quality in a founder of a company they wish to invest in.

CONVERTIBLE NOTES

Many entrepreneurs are confused by *convertible notes*, a common way to finance start-up companies here in Silicon Valley. A convertible note is a financial instrument between a company and investor whereby the investor lends money to the company; this money has an interest-bearing component and has to be repaid at a future date. With respect to start-up investments, a convertible note holder (i.e. investor) has the intention of converting the note into equity in the company at a later date. Most convertible note terms used by start-up companies will convert into equity when the company consummates a qualified financing (typically by a venture capital firm) of an agreed minimum (for example, $1 million).

These convertible notes allow start-up companies to raise smaller amounts of money from investors over time more easily than a larger amount at one time. If there is no conversion (i.e. the start-up company does not achieve a qualified financing), the lenders (i.e. investors) are entitled to have their money, plus interest component, repaid, and if not may be entitled to the company assets.

All entrepreneurs should read the article 'Why Convertible Notes are Sometimes Terrible for Startups' by Mark Suster from GRP. Partners, published on *TechCrunch (techcrunch.com/2012/09/05/ why-convertible-notes-are-sometimes-terrible-for-startups)*. It's one of my favorite articles, and it lists the pros and, more so, cons of convertible notes.

Like many in Silicon Valley, I don't like convertible notes. They don't allow investment deals to be priced at a fixed valuation when the money is raised or the convertible note is *uncapped* (meaning: there is no valuation set on the company). Convertible notes offer flexibility for start-up founders to commence their business by having money deposited into their bank account and leaves the pricing component for a VC to sort out; a 20-percent discount is typically applied to convertible note holders. Yet it leaves both the entrepreneur and VC horribly exposed.

For the inexperienced entrepreneur, they can get caught out. I've seen this time and time again in Silicon Valley, where entrepreneurs get fooled into a false sense of their self-worth as a team, technology and company. Convertible notes are great when the market is bullish, yet when the value of a company falls the entrepreneur loses by having to give up more equity when the deal is eventually priced. More than this, it represents uncertainty to the entrepreneur, who becomes able to spend time not focused on building the business but taking meetings to raise chunks of $25,000 to $50,000 per investor. That's *hand-to-mouth* fundraising and dysfunctional for the company founders. I've seen entrepreneurs start to get caught up in chasing $20,000 high-profile angel investors so they can then drop their name into the next investor pitch.

I received an email from an entrepreneur raising a seed round in 2012, stating that Matt Mullenweg had invested in his company. Matt Mullenweg is well known in Silicon Valley as the founder of WordPress (which provides free blogs and website platforms). The entrepreneur was almost boasting in the email, which, to me, shows the company had lost focus!

Since 2010, Silicon Valley start-ups have started to think and act like budding Hollywood scriptwriters looking to attract A-listers to improve the prospects of their venture.

Entrepreneurs should remember that having Eric Schmidt (ex-CEO of Google and billionaire) invest in your start-up or an A-list angel investor like Reid Hoffman (founder of LinkedIn) invest $25,000 is like the normal person pushing a quarter into a gumball machine at Walgreens! It's inconsequential to them and entrepreneurs that focus on stacking their *cap table* (Silicon Valley slang, short for the 'capital table' and referring to the list of shareholders) with high-profile investors are often deluded and should be more focused on their own future success.

Convertible notes also breed complacency with entrepreneurs. It affords them immediate cash flow often unaccompanied by strict governance — which means they don't have to hit certain milestones in the way they would if there was a fixed priced equity round of capital raised. Being able to take in $25,000 to $50,000 parcels of money up until $500,000 to $750,000 allows the start-up entrepreneur to move the goalposts with previous investors. It allows them to move the targets and milestones around in conversations with investors, and that often creates a lack of confidence and different versions of the same investment presentation.

The bottom line is that entrepreneurs should not get suckered into uncapped convertible notes and put themselves at risk of dilution if future valuations fall.

How VCs can Help with Start-Up Marketing

All start-up entrepreneurs try and *bake in* (a Silicon Valley term for including a technology piece) a viral component to their business model. Founders think long and hard about how to make their product really popular with the type of virality enjoyed by LinkedIn, Instagram, Facebook and Pinterest. It is the holy grail for entrepreneurs and VCs alike to find that their technology is adopted at exponential growth rates.

An interesting insight came to me when I met Sequoia Capital's marketing director, Mark Dempster, and his marketing manager Christy Ikezi in their Sand Hill Road offices in 2009 to discuss how best to optimize and redesign the Sequoia Capital (*www.sequoiacap. com*) website. A friend of mine, Andrew Shotland, introduced me, as he was previously vice president of product and business development at Insider Pages (*www.insiderpages.com*), which Sequoia had funded and was subsequently acquired by IAC, who operate Citysearch (*www.citysearch.com*).

At some point during the meeting, I gained important insight into how VCs work. They like to work through their network and feel more secure that they are getting the best talent this way. Perhaps they'll have less chance of a failed relationship with an external party, as you are a friend of the firm. While this is not a new business practice, it shows the inner circle of how Silicon Valley operates.

Sequoia wanted to showcase their clients, the founders of their portfolio companies and create a website that was different from other venture firms. I strongly doubt it was my idea to create the search function on their current website, yet I certainly did provide a business case for which high audience keywords they should focus on in their search engine optimization. I knew that there was a lot of keyword searches on Google for various terms related to venture capital. I was also aware that no VC in Silicon Valley had really concentrated on keyword optimization in search engines like Google, Bing and Yahoo! on non-branded keywords.

During this meeting at Sequoia, I learned that it is the partial responsibility of the VC's marketing team to assist, where possible, with providing marketing support to their portfolio companies.

As an entrepreneur, you might find that it is a good idea to get in touch with the marketing manager at the venture firms and pitch them on putting you in touch with one of their portfolio firms. Of course, this is assuming your product or service suits their portfolio companies, but it is definitely worthwhile exploring before going directly to their partners to pitch your business.

Back in 2009, I received an email from Katie Belding, vice president of marketing at Norwest Venture Partners, a large venture capital firm here in Palo Alto. Upon meeting with her and Sharon McKenzie in Norwest's marketing group, I realized they were interested in how to get their portfolio companies higher up in search engine rankings. This is primarily what SearchForecast, my website development company, had worked on with several of their portfolio companies. To my surprise, they were very forthcoming in introducing SearchForecast to other of their portfolio companies.

For entrepreneurs, it is important to understand that VC firms can provide free marketing services for your start-up. Don't forget that part of a venture capital firm's mission is to help advance their investment portfolio companies by making introductions to leading edge vendor technologies. This is one way to get exposure to Silicon Valley venture capital firms, and can eventually lead to a partner of the firm, who sits on the board of the company they funded, finding out about your business.

CROWDSOURCING
VIDEO VIRAL FINANCING

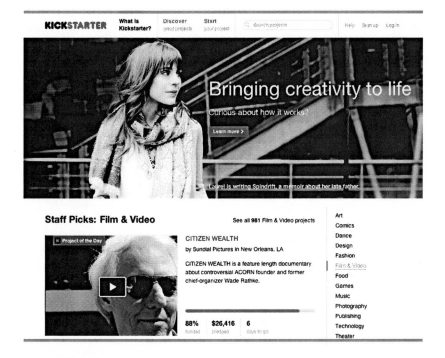

Crowdsourcing venture funding has become extremely popular and, according to several VCs I know, amounted to almost $1.5 billion in 2012. That represents 0.5 percent to one percent of venture capital invested in the USA and clearly illustrates the demand and liquidity of smaller contributors to innovation. With Kickstarter, IndieGoGo and other crowdsourced fundraising platforms, the viral element is helping raise some serious money for start-ups. Fueled by professional yet personal videos from founders, there is a flourishing financing opportunity that didn't exist in Silicon Valley less than four years ago.

When I was studying economic history and public finance at The University of Melbourne in the early 1990s, I learned about the *tontine*, a capital finance scheme used by the Italians and then King Louis XIV of France who used them in the 1600s to finance his armies. I feel that crowdsourcing/funding schemes like Kickstarter (*www.kickstarter.com*) are the modern-day Silicon Valley equivalent of the *tontine*. I've been watching and analyzing those who raised the most money on Kickstarter, and it appears that those who have a great video that stirs up public emotion and impassions the crowd to act are doing best. People respond to the company founder talking passionately about his or her product and team

I encourage you to take a look at the successful pre-sales campaign videos by Pebble, the start-up company that has raised the most money at the time of writing (US$10,266,845), and Lockitron (US$2,278,891) on *KickStarter.com.*

Take a moment to watch these videos:

- *www.kickstarter.com/projects/597507018/pebble-e-paper-watch-for-iphone-and-android*
- *www.youtube.com/watch?feature=player_embedded&v=D1L3o88GKew*

It is interesting that the big money raised via crowdsourcing is going to products that are prototyped and the companies are taking pre-sales orders. This is how new housing developments are marketed and financed offline. This is why the video is *so* important. There are some common themes to successful pre-sales campaign videos, and stating your product/company/founders early on in the video is one of those themes.

Let's now look at Wallet TrackR (*www.wallettrackr.com*), who only raised $56,466. Where did they go wrong compared to Pebble or Lockitron? Wallet TrackR's did not state the product/company/

founders at the start of their video; instead, they takes one minute and 43 seconds to get to this. Let's face it, we all have ADD these days. Most people do not have the patience to wait one minute, 43 seconds, to find out why they are watching something.

A *very* interesting data point is that Stick-N-Find (*www.sticknfind. com*) launched *after* Wallet TrackR, yet they destroyed the tiny numbers Wallet TrackR had amassed. I attribute this mainly to their video. Stink-N-Find also talks about the company, founders and product from the get go. See the video that secured Stick-N-Find US$931,970 at *www.indiegogo.com/sticknfind*.

Over lunch in San Francisco in the fall of 2012 with Michael Berolzheimer from Bee Partners, who invested in Indiegogo, we discussed the genesis of these crowdsourcing fundraising platforms. We both agreed the two most important components of all successful raisings using crowdsourced finance is that the founder(s) had a very specific talent or expertise and that then led to the production of a passionately compelling video. Those of us around the Bay Area in California are energized that there is a flourishing financing opportunity that didn't exist in Silicon Valley less than 4 years ago and see it not as a fad but another sector of the venture capital industry on a global basis.

STRATEGIC INVESTORS

VCs typically like to see strategic investors in later-stage rounds such as Series B, C and D. Typically, strategic investors don't invest in Series A investment rounds, mainly due to the business model not being proven or that they have larger customer bases and bigger engineering teams that require more mature companies to engage with.

Competitor companies may join into a venture capital round of financing as strategic investors. For instance, Payfone (*payfone. com*), the New York–based mobile payment technology company, has raised venture capital from Verizon Ventures and Blackberry Partners Fund.

It is very important to remember that strategic investors will want to gain an advantage with an investment that suits their core business. Entrepreneurs should be very careful in taking strategic money, as it often requires greater resources to engage with strategic investors to maximize their engineering collaboration efforts, reseller channel or co-marketing opportunities.

Strategic investors are often called *smart money* (which, in Silicon Valley, describes investment from people who have industry expertise) and can provide strategic value to start-ups in terms of customers and partnerships. However, most VCs will warn start-ups to be very careful about taking in strategic money too early, particularly when they are public companies.

Those of us in Silicon Valley in 2008 watched as eBay sued Craigslist and Craigslist counter-sued eBay. The lawsuits resulted after eBay launched a U.S. version of its Kijiji classifieds site — which competed directly with Craigslist — and started buying online ads steering internet users looking for Craigslist to its own sites. Craigslist then diluted eBay's equity in the company. In September 2010, a Delaware judge ruled that the actions of Craigslist were unlawful, and that the actions taken by Craigslist founders Jim Buckmaster and Craig Newmark had 'breached their fiduciary duty of loyalty'. The judge restored eBay's stake in the company to 28.4 percent from the diluted 24.85 percent. Not all strategic minority investments turn out like this, but it's a recent episode in the Valley that will be remembered for a long time!

Smart entrepreneurs often look for strategic investment to offset the risk of one of their venture capital firms becoming a *Zombie Fund* (a Silicon Valley term to describe a venture fund that has not or cannot raise new funds). In this situation, a venture capital firm may not be able to participate in future rounds of finance and therefore strategic investors can *pony up* (another Silicon Valley term; this one refers to contributing money to a round of finance).

The National Venture Capital Association (*www.nvca.org*) reported in 2012 that only 8.2 percent ($2.1 billion of the $26.5 billion invested by VCs) came from corporate venture capital groups, another name for strategic investor VCs. The NVCA also reported that 15 percent of venture deals in 2012 included a strategic investor.

I have heard strategic investors in Silicon Valley discussing that one of the main reasons corporates invest in technology start-ups is to invest in innovation. They also do so to foster their own ecosystem and not be beholden to what Sand Hill Road VCs invest in.

Corporate Venture Capital Group Investment Analysis 1995 Through Q4 2012

Year	Count of All Venture Capital Deals	Number of Deals with CVC Involvement	Calculated Percentage of Deals with Corporate VC Involvement	$M Average Amount of All VC Deals	$M Average Amount of CVC Participation	Total VC Investment $M	Total CVC Investment $M	Calculated Percentage of Dollars Coming from CVCs
1995	1,894	145	7.7%	4.23	3.01	8,012.6	436.5	5.4%
1996	2,637	224	8.5%	4.30	3.03	11,341.5	679.4	6.0%
1997	3,222	346	10.7%	4.65	2.73	14,974.9	946.2	6.3%
1998	3,733	501	13.4%	5.76	3.44	21,510.5	1,721.8	8.0%
1999	5,605	1190	21.2%	9.81	6.25	54,960.2	7,436.4	13.5%
2000	8,042	1963	24.4%	13.08	7.64	105,205.3	15,002.6	14.3%
2001	4,591	964	21.0%	8.92	4.76	40,974.2	4,587.6	11.2%
2002	3,202	546	17.1%	6.91	3.49	22,129.0	1,907.5	8.6%
2003	3,020	434	14.4%	6.52	2.94	19,679.6	1,277.0	6.5%
2004	3,217	533	16.6%	7.22	2.88	23,235.1	1,535.2	6.6%
2005	3,300	544	16.5%	7.16	2.81	23,612.5	1,526.6	6.5%
2006	3,885	789	20.3%	7.11	3.22	27,607.2	2,541.9	9.2%
2007	4,212	793	18.8%	7.57	3.23	31,875.1	2,557.6	8.0%
2008	4,168	878	21.1%	7.18	3.04	29,946.6	2,669.9	8.9%
2009	3,141	394	12.5%	6.49	3.35	20,383.4	1,319.0	6.5%
2010	3,624	452	12.5%	6.43	4.15	23,319.0	1,876.7	8.0%
2011	3,943	557	14.1%	7.48	3.97	29,479.8	2,211.0	7.5%
2012	3,715	565	15.2%	7.14	3.86	26,527.8	2,178.4	8.2%

Source: PricewaterhouseCoopers/National Venture Capital Association MoneyTree™ Report, Data: Thomson Reuters

It is important for entrepreneurs to be very aware of the motivations of strategic investors and to ask hard questions of them before accepting their money. Strategic investors naturally lean towards how their investment can benefit their own company, leverage their success first and foremost before your success.

WHAT FOUNDERS LEARN IN
BOARD MEETINGS

When I was younger, I never knew the correct answer to the question that VCs often asked: 'Are you going to run the company in the long term?'

I wish someone had told me as I thought there was a right answer. Good news is, there isn't.

Entrepreneurs really don't know what is ahead of them and it's a loaded question asked by VCs that elicits some interesting answers. The best response from an entrepreneur is something along the lines of being of service to the company in the capacity that is most beneficial, as determined by the board of directors.

Entrepreneurs should understand that one in three founders are not the CEO two or three years after the first funding event. From being the founder to becoming the CEO is a natural pathway when you've just raised a seed round of funding, as the team is small. Typically, one founder handles more commercial responsibilities and the other focuses on technology and product.

Running the company is the entrepreneur's responsibility and, apart from monthly board meetings, VCs have a limited amount of executive input into the business. One of the most important traits VCs look for in entrepreneurs is transparency and honesty. This is key to keeping board meetings with VCs constructive. As an entrepreneur, you need to show complete openness, as this leads to trust from VCs.

Whenever I sit in meetings with starts-ups, I ask myself, 'Is this person being honest? Would they lie to shareholders? Would they act with diligence and care in running the company, if they were funded?'

While some entrepreneurs can get past the funding beauty parade and bank the venture deal, their days are numbered if they can't present VCs with boardroom presentations that articulate sales, product timelines, milestones met, growth scenarios, financial forecasts and cash flow analysis. Monthly presentations to VCs by the founders and CEO should be succinct. Fifteen to 20 slides in a presentation for the monthly boardroom presentations is sufficient. If the presentation is too long, VCs can get weary!

Information-sharing should not be confined to monthly boardroom and annual reports, as required by most term sheets. I've seen many entrepreneurs prepare a slightly longer presentation for *minority investors* (investors whose shareholdings are small and aren't board directors). This slide deck might be 25 slides. Most minority investors have information rights as part of standardized shareholders agreements; hence, they have the right to access financial information. It's important for entrepreneurs to treat minority investors with respect and not dismiss them. Too often, I see entrepreneurs who disregard their investors and share minimal information with them. Disgruntled minority shareholders can quickly tell board directors they aren't happy and put pressure on them to have the entrepreneur sidelined or removed. Sending a quarterly presentation is not too onerous and can add value in terms of the recommendations and introductions the smaller investors can bring.

Of course, it's a fine balance — smaller investors often make the most demands, and you do not want to be overloaded with constantly providing detailed reports. And VCs are decisive; they won't spare entrepreneurs the luxury of not providing detailed information and reporting.

Smart entrepreneurs will also keep *friends of the firm* (a Silicon Valley term describing vendors, LinkedIn associates and partners) updated on their venture-funded start-up by sending emails every quarter. This is a great way to informally keep a broader network of people (let's call them *influencers*) updated with the progress of the company.

For example, a close associate, Tim Cadogan — the CEO of OpenX (*www.crunchbase.com/company/openx*), an advertising technology platform based in Pasadena that has raised over $70 million in venture capital — sends out a quarterly email. It is addressed to 'friends of OpenX' and includes a nice mix of company achievements, industry observations and personal reflections. Having done some work with OpenX previously, Tim and I enjoyed a plane ride from Burbank to San Jose back in 2009. He explained the importance of making everyone feel connected and informed about OpenX, and that did not start or stop in the boardroom. CEOs like Tim understand the importance of information-sharing to a broader group involved with the company. I suggest that entrepreneurs take seriously the formal and informal reporting required not only by the board of directors but also by minority investors and, on a less frequent basis, by *friends of the firm*.

Negotiations and Acquisitions

So how do you handle the exit or acquisition? It's a harrowing experience for those lucky enough to experience it. Entrepreneurs need to understand how acquisitions transpire, as these are the eventual goal of a venture-funded company.

When the acquisition offer is unsolicited (whereby an approach is made even though you have not advertised that the business is looking to sell), I suggest you take the call or meeting and then have one of your advisors with you. This ensures that the other staff members are not aware of the conversation, so their work routines aren't disrupted and, importantly, so you can get independent feedback from your non-executive advisor.

If the discussions require a follow-up call or meeting, I suggest that you delegate to the advisor and remain absent from the next meeting or call. This is somewhat unconventional yet, I feel, very effective as it allows you to validate how serious the offer is without becoming personally involved.

If it's an offer from a known party, (meaning that you know the other company executives) you may suggest catching up at the next trade show for lunch if the company is from out of town. I always suggest dealing with offers from known parties in personal, face-to-face meetings in the first instance, as this shows very good faith.

There is typically a premium paid when the acquirer is known, and entrepreneurs want to find out what that is. Is it the technology, key staff or a certain customer segment?

Good faith goes a long way, particularly if there is not an outcome from the negotiations. If the price offered or terms of the acquisition are rejected, you may wish to enter into a licensing agreement or strategic partnership. This is why offers should be handled with personal attention and care. Personalities are the major reason, in my experience, that deals don't go through. Even if you don't like the acquiring company CEO or executive vice president, make sure they like you. That's part of the art of the deal.

I always recommend to entrepreneurs selling to corporations to look beyond the money in negotiations. It's very easy to get hung up on the dollar value of the transaction, and it is human nature that you think your company is worth more than what is being offered. Having been in this position a few times, I have two personal recommendations:

Firstly, remember that 'a bird in the hand is worth two in the bush' — that is, an offer on the table is worth more than an offer that is initially rejected and a next offer that you're waiting for (which might never come!)

Secondly, 'the first offer is always your best offer'. I've lived through the dot-com bubble and bust. I've seen entrepreneurs playing the exit/acquisition poker hand with no aces in their deck! Don't bluff or play like you have a royal flush when you only have bravado and greed. Take the first offer if it is fair and reasonable. You might never get another.

During the negotiations, I believe that if you have concise financial reporting, a solid story on future product development and show genuine excitement (whether you're bluffing or not doesn't matter) to be part of the acquirer's team, or ensure you are going to always be a good part of their alumni and will work in whatever capacity they would like you to, this is going to hold you in very good stead to get the best price.

A board of directors on the acquiring side will want to make sure there is a good feeling among the team and staff being acquired. I always suggest that entrepreneurs in acquisition talks ask for their staff to be given either an increase in wages or additional stock options upon the acquisition. You want to keep the team motivated, particularly if you as the founder are going to have an earn-out period.

During the negotiation stages, you want to keep emails to a minimum. Get on the phone and talk during negotiations. Emails are for receiving offers in writing. During the discussions, paint a picture to the prospective acquirer that you have not discussed this with the team and you have a timeframe within which you would like them to conduct due diligence and or make a formal offer. Most times, an indicative offer or non-binding offer can be made and subject to due diligence, which usually is 30 to 60 days, becomes binding.

I always keep the attorneys out of it. They do a great job in complicating things and racking up larger fees than required. Back in 2001, I negotiated a large joint venture with a UK software company that had raised over $80 million in venture capital, acquiring the rights to Asia Pacific. As I moved through the negotiations, this firm bought in Mallesons (*www.mallesons.com*) and I could see exactly what was going on. The deal was over-lawyered, in my opinion, and I decided I was going to walk away on the deal. I always insist on keeping the lawyers out of the negotiations and keep it between the principals of the company. This is because, during the early discussions, there is a rapport built and the acquirer is trying to win over the target company executives at a personal level. You want to cradle that relationship and not let cold paws of attorneys touch your prey.

When each side is paying their own legal fees, entrepreneurs should know that, when the acquirer brings in their attorneys, they are serious. If you want to walk away from the deal, you can always ask your attorney to step in and complicate the deal so much that it becomes untenable for the acquirer to consummate a transaction. As a smart entrepreneur, you can always leverage your attorney to kill a deal and save you wasting your time on unwinding acquisition and exit conversations.

If you are looking to sell your company, there are a few options. You can always ask a boutique advisory firm in San Francisco, New York, London, Sydney, Boston or Seattle to do this. They typically charge four to six percent of the purchase price and a minimum engagement fee of $50,000 at between three and six months. Before you get to this stage, it's a lot cheaper to have one of your advisors *pimp your ride* (a Silicon Valley term to describe how an advisor will talk to potential acquirers about a start-up).

4

LIVING IN THE VALLEY:
A VC'S PERSPECTIVE

THE CONTRARIAN

The watercolor paintings of Havana adorn the walls of La Bodeguita del Medio, the Cuban restaurant at 463 S. California Avenue in Palo Alto. It's an ideal setting for a casual lunch with Andrew Zeif, a corporate attorney specializing in start-ups from Paradigm Counsel, and Ella van Gool, Senior Vice President of Venture Capital Services from Square 1 Bank, located on Sand Hill Road.

It was a structured lunch to find out what deal size or *appetite* — whether it be angel, seed, Series A, later stage, hybrid, etc. — for investment our syndicate of investors had. *Do you like priced deals? Is co-investment desirable? What technology sectors or segments are preferred?* These are the types of conversations attorneys and bankers have.

As I devoured the spicy fish tacos, I couldn't help but think that entrepreneurs are like the overworked Cuban farmers depicted in the painting on the restaurant wall. Entrepreneurs are mostly oblivious to VCs, attorneys and bankers talking about the size of deals, structure of financing instruments, sectors that are hot and transactional costs. Many young entrepreneurs who have not yet experienced a venture capital funding event are not exposed to these conversations and, equally, most attorneys and bankers have no firsthand experience of being a start-up.

Somewhere in between this lies an impasse for those of us who play in both start-up land and venture-capital land in Silicon Valley. I say 'impasse' because it's where there is friction — friction from entrepreneurs who don't understand the mindsets of bankers, parameters of investors and attorney practices, and resistance from VCs who are trying to understand or get comfortable with an entrepreneur's business model.

This is, in fact, where my contrarian viewpoint has emerged. It's from the gaps between the knowledge of those who are part of the production of start-ups and those who have never experienced it as a founding team member. I listen to people's opinions and suggestions, and then take an opposing view in my mind without expressing an opinion. Quite the opposite, I will purposefully agree with someone about a particular point when I actually may disagree with them, just to tease out their thought process.

It's very easy in Silicon Valley to be wowed by the start-up team, blown away by the technology and dazzled by the investors and advisors. No one packages investment decks better than Bay Area entrepreneurs. That said, you have to create a contrarian view and stop yourself from *drinking the Kool Aid* — an American term for not agreeing with others on how great a start-up company is.

Even the best optimists have to become a contrarian in order to unemotionally evaluate investments — and that applies to both entrepreneurs and investors! VCs are trained to think with their heads, not their hearts. To initially like a business yet be prepared to not like it in the next fleeting thought is the instinct of the VC.

My favorite contrarians are Fred Wilson, who blogs at *fredwilson. vc*; Roger McNamee; Mike Maples, at *rogerandmike.com*; and Marc Andreeson, at *blog.pmarca.com*.

GREEN BANANAS

Trader Joe's (*www.traderjoes.com*) is a local favorite for Valleyites, as the company's retail stores have a neighborly, non-commercial community and organic vibe.

One night, I popped into the Menlo Park store. As I walked in I was met by a large, standing, multi-tiered shelf of bananas. I'm not big on bananas, but they always offer five for a dollar. 'Loss leader,' I thought to myself as I strolled past to grab a large packet of sea salt potato chips and roasted seaweed snacks, which have nourished this road warrior for many late nights over the years. Standing at the checkout,

I saw a VC I know from around the neighborhood. We struck up an idle chitchat while waiting in the queue. He was carrying three of those five-for-a-dollar banana bunches. We talked about various deals and, in particular, one SaaS (software-as-a-service) company that his venture firm had invested in, which was performing solidly but not growing at the exponential rate he had hoped for.

As I got into the car I realized that so many funded start-ups are like those banana bunches he was holding. One was a green bunch. Like software companies, some bananas can be fully grown but not ripe. However, that's why I never buy green bananas: they often never ripen.

THE MOTHER NET

Cheeky Monkey Toys on Santa Cruz Avenue, Menlo Park, is a great shop. Not as good as Hamley's in Oxford Street, London, or FAO Schwartz on 5th Avenue, New York City, but it's about a mile from Sand Hill Road and the toy shop of choice for discerning parents wanting to buy a present of note for a kids birthday party.

In early 2012, I was watching a magic show at here with Brad Murphy, a friend who works at Facebook (and also a Facebook friend) with our respective daughters one Saturday afternoon. We were the only guys in the place, surrounded by 150 mothers and kids. I got to thinking that Facebook was the best magic show in town. It had enthralled venture capitalists for years and it's meteoric growth was catapulted by mothers sharing their family photos. Now it was the biggest IPO of all, raising $16 Billion!

Don't underestimate the power of the Mothers I told myself!

There's a rule at many schools around Silicon Valley that if you're having a birthday party, you have to invite all the kids in the class. At least this is so in primary school grades.

At first glance, this might appear like it's to do with being polite. In reality, it's about networking. You see, Silicon Valley is all about who you know. The real difference between entrepreneurs in Silicon Valley and ROW, the acronym used by Americans to classify the 'rest of world', is not only who you know but the speed at which you can access them.

At our kids school in Menlo Park, there are usually three kinds of people: lawyers and attorneys, brokers or bankers, and executives in both private and publicly listed software companies. So school is, by default, a networking mechanism, and the birthday parties are the informal meeting places. I've often told budding entrepreneurs who are in their early to mid twenties, fresh to Silicon Valley, that there are two 'nets'. The first is the internet, which, powered by so many free Wi-Fi hotspots, makes the Web faster than any other place on the planet. But there is one communication network that is faster, and that is the Mother Net. If you want to get to someone's husband who is a VC or IT executive at Apple or Google, mention something to your wife or a mom of one of your kids' friends. *Bam*, that news will travel faster than a press release to *TechCrunch*. I'm serious. Mothers play a critical part in the well-oiled Silicon Valley networking machine. From organizing Pumpkin Patch festivals to Men's Poker nights, the networking bred into and facilitated by the school systems in Silicon Valley is an ingredient in start-ups that is not known to many outsiders.

I was involved with a video metrics company called GlanceGuide. From the moms and dads within the classroom, the first purchase order from Facebook was organized — all from networking at Starbucks and Peet's after kids drop off at school. I mean, really, how do start-ups from outside Silicon Valley stand a chance? Like so many others, this is why I moved to Palo Alto: to be closer to the opportunities and to seize the chance of being in the right place at the right time.

Even 'native Californians' are not native to Silicon Valley. We are all imports, migrated from South Africa, France, Israel, Australia,

Venezuela or even closer — from Chicago, Miami or even LA. The forcefield that protects and binds those in Silicon Valley is not how super smart we are, but the fact that we are all pioneers who have come to the Valley to seek inspiration and fortune.

You need to come to Silicon Valley to live if you're going to be taken seriously in raising venture capital. The hotel rooms are littered with those who pass through to test the waters. Staying in a Motel 6 or Best Western hotel for a week or two isn't risking it all. These entrepreneurs aren't serious. They want the comforts and security of home. They aren't prepared to risk everything, which is what every one of us has done in moving to Silicon Valley. This is why people here are happy to help and are sensitive to introduce you to someone who can help you. They are aware that you need help because they too have come from far away to be here. This is the fabric of networking in Silicon Valley.

VCs often say on their websites or in person that they don't invest outside of California. That doesn't just preclude England, Australia or Sweden; I'm talking about Nevada, Omaha and Texas, too. Why? VCs are typically married and don't want to travel. Some of my regular golf partners are married with kids, and cringe at the thought of going to Boston, New York or Austin to visit portfolio companies. It's just too far. Lots of venture capitalist cringe at driving up the 101 from Sand Hill Road to the City of San Francisco in peak hour is bad enough, let alone the delays of domestic US air travel.

Entrepreneur in Residence

Every person working in Silicon Valley has a great job. Even low-level developers get paid six figures for coding in start-ups! It's become so competitive here in Silicon Valley since 2007 to find talent that many start-ups set up offices in Seattle, Austin or New York and, in other cases, companies are acquired just to get the talent. This is called an *acqui-hire* — what we in Silicon Valley use to indicate the acquisition of a start-up, which is roughly equivalent to the VC's investment plus a small premium (say, 20 to 30 percent). These acqui-hires have grown in frequency since 2011, as the abundance of start-ups unable to move from seed investment to Series A is increasing while finding engineering talent in the Bay Area has become more difficult.

It's hard to think of a better job than being an EIR (short for Entrepreneur in Residence), which is typically a six to twelve month stint at a VC firm. There is often no remuneration for being an EIR, usually because this position is offered to a founder or senior executive of a portfolio company previously funded by the venture firm. This company has usually been acquired and the founder or executive is invited by the venture firm to spend their days looking at investment opportunities or, more to the point, sit in investment pitch meetings.

My advice to entrepreneurs is to check to see if an EIR is listed on the VC's website. They are often approachable outside of their formal position and may even answer a well-written email request via the premium paid email service offered by LinkedIn.

A friend of mine, Michael Buhr, who worked at eBay in corporate development, became an EIR at Shasta Ventures in 2009. Over coffee at Peet's one morning, Michael was recalling the difficulty that even well-known VCs have in finding great investment deals. We started talking about the number of VCs in Silicon Valley, which in recent years is rumored to have reached over 5000 (counting angel investors). Now, with 5,000 investors and thousands of start-ups being seeded or funded in some way, we concluded that, despite all the money, big-name venture partners and close proximity, there is a degree of serendipity that goes with meeting the next big start-up company. Michael pointed to a table in the back of Peet's and said, 'That's where I met the Pinterest founders when they were very early in their business.' Michael looked at me blankly and, with a wry smile, said, 'Who knew!'

And that's Silicon Valley in a nutshell.

You never know where and when you're going to meet the next big-deal company in Silicon Valley. And even if you are a venture partner or EIR on Sand Hill Road, the local coffee shop is just as serendipitous a meeting place these days. Some EIRs find going to an office stifling, while others enjoy the structure.

In 2010, Eric Ries, author of the very insightful book *The Lean Start Up*, and I were having coffee at Starbucks on Santa Cruz Avenue, Menlo Park. He told me he felt a little strange about being referred to in the local press as a 'venture advisor' to Kleiner Perkins, a very well-respected venture capital firm. Eric is passionate about helping start-ups and said he felt constrained as a perceived advisor to just one venture capital firm. He's now doing a great job teaching start-ups how to be lean, perhaps something you can't always do inside a venture capital firm.

I suppose the formal EIR process is still entrenched, yet there is a greater fluidity and opportunities for investors to view start-ups in Silicon Valley than ever before. In many ways, the larger venture firms are feeling squeezed out of the smaller Series A rounds and have started to invest alongside accelerator groups. For instance, Sierra Ventures, the billion-dollar Sand Hill Road venture fund, puts in $80,000 into start-ups selected by Angel Pad (*angelpad.org*) to ensure they get access to smaller investments. That was unheard of in years past.

The only time I had ever heard of larger VCs putting small amounts of money to work was when a partner would write a start-up a personal check because it was too small an amount for their larger venture capital fund to invest in or they invested into smaller *feeder venture funds*. One such smaller fund is run by a great guy, Gady Nemirovsky of Inspiration Ventures (*www.inspirationvc.com*)

— a $20 million fund that boasts notable Sand Hill Road VCs as their limited partners. Gady is a successful serial entrepreneur himself. I have been on calls with Gady where he has told entrepreneurs not to raise money. That is refreshing advice to hear and comes from a very well-qualified person who has been on both sides of the table.

OFF THE RADAR

For as long as I can remember, DealMaker Media has produced the *Under The Radar* conference (*www.undertheradarblog. com*), which is a great event to see new companies pitch and in a casual environment and meet VCs. It's well attended even among the avalanche of innovation days and Pitchfest events that happen every other week in Silicon Valley.

Yet the most effective angel investors I've met are those who stay off the radar. They work in the background and prefer to stay away from the spotlight cast on celebrity investors. The rise of celebrity angel investing here in the Valley which was largely heralded by *TechCrunch*, running articles on how the inner circle of angel investors collaborated and profiling them at Sunday morning brunches or closed room dinners. In 2010, Michael Arrington from *TechCrunch* reported on where angel investors meet regularly — google it and have a read.

While no-one can condone secret meetings and collusion for rumoured fixing pricing of valuations, entrepreneurs should know that most VCs typically refer start-ups raising money to other VCs when they are actually going to invest or have already invested in that company. It's rare in my experience to see investors wasting their time to recommend a company to another venture partner in a different firm when they are not investing. It's just how VCs in the Valley work. It's normal protocol not to *flick deals* to other investors without being an existing investor or having committed to invest in the current round of funding. The only exception is where the company raising money falls outside of a VC firm's investment focus.

With investors being showcased on stage at conferences like Vator Splash (*vator.tv*) and *TechCrunch* Disrupt (*techcrunch.com/events*), the trend for many experienced angel investors is to go the other way. By that, I mean retreat from any spotlight or crowded room. Remember: the best investors are not looking in the crowd for opportunities. They are often loners, looking at new markets that aren't crowded. They swim against the tide and feign conventional trends. This is where the new technology opportunities lie. Many angel investors were and still are entrepreneurs and often still working in technology companies.

So is the Valley becoming too crowded? Maybe. There's a feeling among some angel investors in Silicon Valley that the next wave of big companies will be born outside of Silicon Valley. While several of the larger Sand Hill Road venture firms have had offices in Israel and India for some years now, there are initiatives like Geeks on a Plane (*geeksonaplane.com*), which is organized by Silicon Valley–based 500 Start-Ups, and iconic angel investors like Peter Thiel investing $12 million into the New Zealand–based Valar Ventures (*www.valarventures.com*), which points to the flow of serious angel investors and their money outside of the Valley.

It's also happening at the smaller angel investor level. Thanks to San Francisco–based Ariel Poler, a well-known and respected angel investor, entrepreneurs from outside of Silicon Valley can now access Best of Angel (*bestofangel.com*). This website, which Ariel established, allows entrepreneurs from anywhere in the world to create a pitch deck using script and video templates and guidelines that are in a shape and form that Silicon Valley investors like.

I got to know Ariel, working with him on sites like *Bills.com* and *Speeddate.com*. He's one of the sharper tools in the Silicon Valley shed. Given his international experience and Venezuelan heritage, Ariel understands that there are amazing start-up investment opportunities outside of Silicon Valley that are often unheard of due to lack of access to local investors.

All of this affirms the recognition by Silicon Valley investors that, despite the popular mindset that the best companies in the world come to the Valley eventually (think: Facebook and Pinterest in recent times), there hasn't been, until now, a lot of outreach of investors and money moving to find foreign entrepreneurs outside of the Valley. Of course, this has been fueled in part by valuations being too high in Silicon Valley and partly due to the nature of the VCs wanting to find new pastures, invest in new frontiers and tap new marketplaces of opportunity.

The universe is expanding for start-ups, and investors are traversing the globe looking for the next big thing. Eventually, however, the successful start-ups move to Silicon Valley to access additional venture capital, management expertise, growth into the US market and larger exit multiples!

THE STANFORD DISH

When I first moved to Silicon Valley, I noticed there were not as many sidewalks on the roads. In fact, if you come from Europe or Australia, you immediately notice the lack of public transport as well. The 'Cal Train' (*www.caltrain.com*) is the only train line, and it runs from San Francisco down to San Jose. Can you believe that? It's true. Check out the stations where the only train in Silicon Valley stops: *www.caltrain.com/stations/systemmap.html.*

Not that this matters much, because cars are quite cheap in the Valley and there has been a surge in carpooling websites and ride-sharing apps in recent years — see, for example, Lyft (*www.lyft.me*) and SideCar (*www.side.cr*). So it's not hard to get a cheap ride with others going in your direction, or even a quicker service with the private drivers that Uber (*www.uber.com*) offers.

Like many professionals in the Valley, I like to break the cycle of conference calls, coffee shop meetings and boardroom presentations with an outside walk. It helps me think and unwind. A bunch of us often walk around 'The Dish' up on Junipero Serra Boulevard behind Stanford University. The Dish is a surreal setting overlooking Portola Valley, a small town of 5000 residents to the west of the Interstate 280 and Sand Hill Road, the home of the eminent VCs. On the east side, you can see the terracotta roof tiles of the Stanford University faculty buildings amid the California oaks that blend into the green Silicon Valley landscape as it stretches out to the San Francisco Bay.

Walking around The Dish is a kaleidoscope of start-ups, visible from the names of their companies on their T-shirts or hoodies as you pass by fellow walkers. I often wonder if walking around The Dish is a way for start-ups to promote their companies. It's a good idea, too, because there are lots of Stanford students walking around the circuit as well.

On a walk in October 2012, private investor Josiah Hornblower was telling me about his biotech company after a $17 million grant it received from the Government of Texas. As part of the deal, he was relocating the company to Austin, Texas. Austin has gained popularity in recent years as an outpost for technology companies who find more attractive labor costs and lower costs of living.

As Josiah and I walked past two Stanford students, it was the first time I heard the term 'snapchatting', which one of the girls used to describe how one of her college dorm buddies had sent her a photo instead of text messaging. In December 2012 and early 2013,

Snapchat (*www.snapchat.com*) announced a $8.5 million round and Series A of $13.5 million led by Benchmark Capital.

Growing up in Melbourne, Australia, I walked around the Royal Botanical Gardens (locals call it 'The Tan'). Having spent a lot of time in New York, I also enjoy walking through Central Park, often passing by Strawberry Fields and, when possible, from the Marble Arch end of Hyde Park in London down to Kensington Palace and back.

The 3.5 miles around The Dish for many years have involved discussions with entrepreneurs and or with VCs. Walking and talking is a great way to exercise and learn. The Dish is a mecca for those in the Valley and, for those reading this book who have not walked around The Dish, be sure to do so with a potential start-up founder, advisor, friends, venture partner or staff at your technology company.

Among the frenetic pace of grueling seven-day-a-week work schedules, The Dish is an oasis for all of us here inside Silicon Valley and a beautiful environment that keeps us healthy in mind and body.

READING THE TEA LEAVES

Silicon Valley seems to have an inordinate number of palm and tarot card readers. They are everywhere. As you drive through the downtowns from San Jose through Mountain View up to San Francisco, the blue, red and green neon lights that bulge in the small, dark shop windows catch your eye. At Café Venetia on University Avenue, I was hearing an entrepreneur pitch while, at the table less than six feet away, the tarot card reader was performing his ritual.

VCs also have their modern-day equivalents of psychic insights. I call it 'reading the tea leaves' and, in many ways, it's an instinct they get before making a decision about investing in a company. This helps the necessary background-checking involved in venture-capital investing and assists in imagining scenarios on how the company will look in the future.

I'm always telling entrepreneurs to model out scenarios to help VCs read the tea leaves. Over lunch at Jin Sho, a Japanese restaurant on California Avenue in Palo Alto, Steve Bennet, adjunct faculty at San Jose State and active angel investor, and I were engaged in hearing about this exciting Bay Area company in the iPad Point of Sale space, which was growing really fast. In two years, the company had hit $5 million in revenue, taken $4 million in venture capital and, as Steve explained (wearing his part-time CFO hat for this company), they needed a mix of debt and equity to take out some disruptive minority shareholders. I began to read the tea leaves.

Many subscribe to the notion that you should never invest in a company where your venture capital is being used to pay out minority investors. They need to keep some skin in the game, and this is often done using warrants that are struck to exercise on exit. The conversation between myself, Steve and a few other VCs at the table consisted of quizzing why minority investors would want to take an early exit at the same valuation they invested in. Had they lost faith in the founders? Perhaps they were young with limited domain experience. Was it that the competitors had raised more money and another company was recently acquired? Or was their technology inferior and, as a result, couldn't scale?

As the conversation buzzed into 'what if' scenarios, the VC were fundamentally assessing risk. We were balancing up management team versus the market size, competitor activity versus capital-raising needs. Basically, how could this company become a market leader? Like so many calibrations and mental arithmetic done by

VCs when talking about start-ups, a lot has to do with determining how things will pan out. As the tea leaves were settling in each VC's cup, my mind cast back to the last time Steve and I sat at a restaurant munching on Spider Sushi rolls.

It was early 2006 and I'd met Steve for lunch when he had just taken a part-time CFO role at *iControl.com*: a fledging software start-up to help secure homes via web browsers. At that time, iControl had raised some seed money and needed to get big or go home. Steve was telling me that Sand Hill Road VCs were not receptive. The mood in 2007 was pretty glum among VCs. There were a handful of IPOs and, while mobile start-ups were getting funded, there was no sense of urgency on Sand Hill Road. A few months later, I received an email update saying Charles River Ventures and Intel Ventures had invested $5 million. Two years later, John Doerr, the legendary VC and partner at Kleiner Perkins Caulfield & Byers, joined the board of directors at iControl after leading a $15.5 million Series B round.

And then my mind cleared, the virtual tea leaves settled in my consciousness, and I realized that the difference between this company we were discussing being successful or not, given everything else being equal, was the VC connections that Steve had in getting it financed in a Series B round. You see, like the internet, Silicon Valley is a network. VCs can strongly influence the winner, as often the speed at which a trusted person can get to them is the difference between a start-up being successful or not. I knew that, at some point, this market of using iPad Point of Sale would become an *arms race* (which, in Silicon Valley, means a competitive situation whereby start-ups have reached equal footing on their technology and the winner raises more money and outspends the other on product, marketing, distribution, etc.).

iControl went on to raise another $23 million in a Series C round and $50 million in a Series D round, totaling $93 million in five years. I decided that Steve was the linchpin in this company, and that it is not just a great product and team that wins the day but rather the speed of access to venture capital at pivotal times.

What Steve Jobs Did for Entrepreneurs

As most of us living in and around Palo Alto know, Steve Jobs lived in relative modesty. In May 2010, I saw him at the CVS Pharmacy at the Town & Country shopping center on El Camino Real in Palo Alto — no frills, airs or graces as he strolled past me and my daughter, enjoying our Saturday morning coffee at Mayfield Bakery.

'There's the guy from the Apple website,' my seven-year daughter said with excitement. She didn't realize it was Steve Jobs but knew his face from videos from the Apple website. She rushed in after him and I scurried off to grab her!

What I noticed as I approached Anneliese, who had got down the same aisle as Steve, was that he wasn't wearing a watch, just his faded denim jeans, black long-sleeve T-shirt and trainers. Just a humble person, picking up a prescription from the pharmacy.

In my opinion, his disinterest in material goods and trimmings of wealth are the real legacy that he left to the younger generation. As the Apple comeback story surged on a global scale off the back of staggering iPhone and iPod sales, the world learned of the real Steve Jobs: a man driven by perfection and not by his assets or bank balance.

On October 6, 2011, the day after Steve Jobs passed away, my kids had a dental appointment at 10am. The appointment was one mile from Steve Jobs's house in Palo Alto, so on the way back I drove them down Waverley Street, where his house is situated. I was flooded with a freeze-frame of his thin legs and bare wrist with no watch that day at CVS Pharmacy. It all happened so fast in his 56 years, and perhaps that's why he didn't wear a watch.

At lunch recently in Left Bank on Santa Cruz Avenue, Menlo Park, a VC in his late 50s was talking about how the younger generation of entrepreneurs in Silicon Valley are motivated by wealth but have more of a social capital awareness and a desire to do good beyond just making money. The ideals of Silicon Valley, given its 40- or 50-year history, are still being molded, and I feel that Steve Jobs is a pillar upon which the future of entrepreneurship will be built. After a certain amount, it's not about the money but being the best you can be — to achieve perfection and strive for something beyond monetary compensation, and to distill a feeling of innovation in the world.

Every time you touch an Apple device, like that which I'm writing this book on, you can feel the impact that the man had on so many people. Today fifty percent of US households have an Apple product.

Organizations like The Full Circle Fund (*fullcirclefund.com*) and Causes (*causes.com*) are two examples of how Silicon Valley entrepreneurs can contribute as a social entrepreneur. In many ways, sites like Kickstarter (*www.kickstarter.com*) is also a venture capital embodiment of how people can be more socially conscious and participate in causes to change lives.

THE SOCIAL CONSCIOUS MOVEMENT

It wasn't just Steve Jobs who made it cool to be more socially conscious. Around the time of the first iPhone launch in June 2007, when Steve Jobs was propelled to geek stardom, the film *An Inconvenient Truth* starring Al Gore also created a platform for social responsibility among entrepreneurs in Silicon Valley.

I first heard of Al Gore in the early 1990s as the US vice president associated with the phrase 'information superhighway'. Having started my first internet company while at the University of Melbourne in 1993, I read his speeches and knew he was a man of vision. I watched him graciously accept defeat in the 2000 US presidential election campaign, then win international praise for his climate change mantra and accept the 2007 Nobel Peace Prize.

So when I had the pleasure of meeting Al Gore over lunch in December 2007 at Paragon, a restaurant on 2nd Street in San Francisco, I mentioned that I hoped we could work on something together one day. Al told me he needed our help in saving the planet. I said I would keep an eye out for good green-tech start-ups and let him know.

VCs inside the Valley tell me that Kleiner Perkins has put around 40 percent of their funds in 2007 towards green-tech. I'm not sure whether this is true, but Al Gore became an investment partner in the Sand Hill Road Venture Capital firm Kleiner Perkins Caulfield & Byers.

When I met Tom Arnold, cofounder of a start-up company called Gridium at Café Borrone, in El Camino, Menlo Park, in March 2012, he looked really similar to a young Al Gore. Tom and his co-founder Adam Stein had the same passion to change the world of commercial property owners who were not in control of reducing their energy bills because they lacked the information on energy demand. In April 2012, Arafura Ventures, for which I'm a partner, invested in Gridium. Today, Gridium delivers simple-to-use energy analysis software to help thousands of commercial property managers track and reduce their energy spending. Gridium's SnapMeter technology reads energy data from smart meters and ties together energy demand, tariff information, local weather data, the square footage and occupancy of buildings to provide help property owners reduce energy output.

In small ways, we can change the world. I see many young entrepreneurs today being more socially conscious than ever before.

Young entrepreneurs want to create cultures inside their start-ups that aim to give back to the community. Technology is bringing together people from all over the world via blogs, tweets, photo sharing and videos. This is creating less boundaries between cultures and improving the global consciousness in social values as we begin to understand each other.

GRASSROOTS AND THE BLOCK

I didn't quite understand the meaning of the Jennifer Lopez song 'Jenny from the Block' until I moved to Palo Alto in Silicon Valley and was invited to a block camping trip at Lake Tahoe. *The block*, for the information of all of us non-Americans, is a term that refers to the street you live on and, more generally, the neighborhood you are from. The nice thing about Silicon Valley is that there is a great sense of community, and many people on the street or avenue you live on have neighborly barbecues, Fourth of July parties and, in my block's case, an annual camping trip to Lake Tahoe.

As we sat underneath the stars on that summer's night, singing along to one of the Google engineers' rendition of 'Kumbaya', my friend Bob Plaschke, founder and CEO of Sonim Technologies (makers of the world's most rugged phone), told me something I'll never forget: 'You see, Marc, in Silicon Valley we're a close community of folks who are very grassroots. Very few of us make the superstar club, but along the way we make close friends and watch each other's backs.'

It is the block that creates the foundation of the community in Silicon Valley and, like in most communities in the world, provides an architecture of trust built by the goodwill of those in the community. It is the block that we go home to each night after battling inside start-ups and venture-backed companies.

The block is friendly, a sanctuary away from the pressures of commercial reality, where a glass of wine, a smiling face and genuine neighborhood community renew the spirit of innovation.

So to all the budding entrepreneurs thinking of coming to Silicon Valley from neighborhoods that don't interact or barely speak to each other, be prepared for a change. It's good for business, as, while your neighbors aren't working in your start-up, they are always willing to hear what you do and genuinely happy to help. It's a real network that you can leverage without feeling like you're over reaching. So get involved with your block, accept invitations to even the smallest neighborhood event, and socialize — it's a great way to build networks and a fantastic place to get personal introductions to VCs, clients and trusted advisors.

Demonstrating thought leadership is important for entrepreneurs, not only among your peer group to attract other likeminded co-founders or early employees to the start-up, but also to encourage referral sales. While blogging and tweeting by founders is important to demonstrate thought leadership, there is perhaps no better way to project your company name to the masses than to advertise on a billboard on the US 101 interstate highway between San Francisco and San Jose.

My good friend David Rodnitzky, founder/CEO of PPC Associates (*ppcassociates.com*), a search engine marketing company based in

San Mateo, took out a $20,000-a-month billboard on the US 101 between Ralston Avenue and Hillsdale Boulevard in January 2013. A billboard on the 101 doesn't just expose your company to hundreds of thousands of eyeballs; it's also a statement that the business is developed to the point of not just being a start-up and having the capacity to take on the bigger guys.

Perhaps one of the better advertisers leveraging the US 101 billboards is Box (*www.box.com*), who have had several billboards in 2012 that focused on contrasting their cloud-sharing and storage services with SharePoint, a main competitor.

If you're a start-up with something to say, the US 101 is a great place to advertise. Being controversial and antagonistic is part of the creative swagger. It sends a clear message to Valley-ites that your start-up is challenging the status quo and is a company to be taken seriously.

A billboard on the US 101 is often a milestone for entrepreneurs as it shows decision makers in Silicon Valley that the company is *ready for primetime*. As a shareholder of AdSemble (*www.adsemble. com*) based here in Silicon Valley, I have first hand insights into how entrepreneurs can promote on digital signage screens in high traffic areas.

Matthew Olivieri, CEO and Founder of AdSemble advises entrepreneurs and start-up tech companies not to advertise until they are ready.

5

THE FUTURE IS NOW

THE CHINESE CASH SYNDICATES

I like *The New York Times*. Its articles have a nice balance of culture, art and science that smooth out the often one-dimensional views and nerdy techie conversations that Silicon Valley folks have. With the US dollar depreciating against other currencies since 2006 and after the subprime meltdown and mortgage crisis in the USA, there has been a slew of articles on Chinese investors pouring money into commercial real estate and Manhattan luxury apartments.

Around the time of the Facebook IPO in May 2012, there were a lot of real estate agents rubbing their mitts together, thrilled at the expectant millionaires pumping up house prices in Silicon Valley. It turned out it wasn't social media's early employees buying houses. Rather, it was Chinese investors who had been piling into the residential real estate market in Silicon Valley and — get this — paying cash for houses.

I confirmed this rumor with my Chinese acupuncturist in Menlo Park and some other friends in tech companies who live in the neighborhood. Amazing! Chinese investors are pooling $50,000 cash bundles (about the amount they could legally take from China) and forming syndicates to buy apartments and houses for cash. Maybe they had been doing it before I found out, but imagine if they start doing this in the start-up angel market.

Could this actually happen?

I rang my good friend Judy Citron, real estate agent to the Silicon Valley movers and shakers, who told me that in December 2012 she had listed a property in Palo Alto for $2 million; cash only and bids would be accepted within five days. The house was listing in the morning, had fourteen showings by the afternoon and three offers that evening. The house was sold by 11am the following day. Judy was stunned. I was intrigued. Judy told me a local Chinese buyer got the property, overbid the Google engineers and trumped the surgeon's bid by several hundred thousand! That, my friends, is Silicon Valley: where new financing is happening in real time!

While America sits around watching six-hour games of NFL football and four-hour baseball games and socializing on Facebook, the Chinese mainlander is working and pooling money to buy the houses in the area. Don't say I didn't warn you America!

THE 'I' GENERATION

'Facebook's for old people,' is what my fifth-grade daughter said as she was taking a photo of her buddies outside the Sugar Shack in Menlo Park. 'It's Instagram, Dad.' As she uploaded the photo to Instagram she revealed that now she had were over 200 followers. It was January 2013, and less than six months after Facebook acquired Instagram the game had been changed by the kids who 'insti' (short for Instagram) and the 'i' Generation: the kids who use photos on Instagram to express themselves and network socially as opposed to texting or posting messages on Facebook walls.

That's how fast Silicon Valley can change the world. Instagram was launched in October 2010 here in Palo Alto, and as I write this the service has 100 million active users per month.

Recently, at an Apple Genius Bar appointment at Stanford Mall, my daughter was taking photos and instagramming with friends when the Apple technician said to me, 'You're slowing her down,' as I was interrupting my daughter with conversation. That was true: snapchatting with Instagram had greater efficiencies than talking or plain texting. It's a deeper and richer form of communication. I was slowing her down. I just needed someone from Apple to tell me!

It made me think that, while Generation Y will sit at a table of people and feel the incessant need to feel connected and keep up to date with other people's news, Generation I is about expressing the richness in their lives by taking photos of themselves and things that matter to them. A major part of the credibility and respect from the network of Instagram friends comes from the quality of pictures taken. Kids in Silicon Valley are making friends with different age groups at school and kids from within the neighborhood via Instagram and photo sharing. The longer-term impact of this is that it creates a very visual generation that is articulate as voyeurs with wider circles of friends.

I've seen this flow from Instagram into iMovie, with many kids in Silicon Valley bypassing PowerPoint and moving to movie-editing software on their computers. If you think about it, this is a logical extension of the image-curation process in a video form. Videos taken using iPods and smartphones are stitched together in iMovie to create visual photo albums.

I'm not worried that kids wont be able to express themselves; I'm excited that they can enrich their lives by taking photos and sharing with friends how it makes them feel. The 'i' Generation are mobile, photo-centric, and communicate with snapchats more regularly than their parents update Facebook and talk on mobile phones.

Don't Look Back

We're a progressive lot in Silicon Valley. Historical tours are nonexistent. We don't look back that often. There is an incredible excitement here in the Valley that this generation is making history. Publishing platforms like Blogger, Wordpress, YouTube, Twitter, Facebook, Instagram, Snapchat, and Pinterest are allowing people to load the World Wide Web with stories and photos at epic proportions. We're capturing the future every day.

It's in the make-up or DNA of those in the Valley. I first realized this on Easter Saturday morning in 2005 at Holbrook Palmer Park on

Watkins Avenue in Atherton, right in the heart of Silicon Valley. The annual Easter egg hunt had commenced with a crowd of 400 parents and kids, running across the two-acre park. As the crowd sprinted off to find chocolate goodies, a three-year-old girl was crying. She had been left alone at the start line. 'Where are her parents?' I asked several people. I picked up the girl, carried her over to a policeman and informed him that she was left behind and that her parents must be among the crowd looking for Easter eggs 300 yards away.

Within minutes, a somewhat unperturbed mother ran up to the policeman, who reunited lost child with parent. I bit my lip and shrugged my shoulders when I noticed the basket full of Easter eggs hanging from the mother's forearm. The cop could feel my bewilderment, turned to me after mother and daughter were ten feet away and said, 'She must be in technology; those people never look back.'

That story sticks in my mind, and it's true. People look *forward* in Silicon Valley, not back, and that is something that is very important. Silicon Valley has such a short history that, in many ways, people don't consider the past and just focus on the future.

In February 2013, a documentary called *Silicon Valley* aired on PBS. It documents how Robert Noyce, who invented the integrated circuit and cofounded Intel, started the Silicon Valley culture of entrepreneurship and fueled the revolution we find ourselves in today. The video is available at *video.pbs.org/video/2332168287* and is a must-watch.

* * *

When I first got to Silicon Valley, one of my neighbors had a row of orange trees along his front fence. I'd put Cassie, my youngest daughter up on my shoulders and we'd pick the fruits. My other neighbor had their plum tree drop hundreds of plums onto our lawn in two to three weeks around May–June. Another neighbor had a persimmon tree. I didn't know what a persimmon was let alone that they grew on trees! You see, Silicon Valley was full of fruit farms, and its very mild, warm temperature, with few windy days, makes it ideal for producing silicon.

I hope one day soon the thought leaders of Silicon Valley give more thought to building a museum to showcase the historical achievements of companies like Microsoft, Apple, Intel, Cisco, HP, Adobe, Juniper Networks, Google, Facebook, eBay and many more. The Computer History Museum (*www.computerhistory.org*) on Shoreline Boulevard in Mountain View is fantastic to visit, yet there should be more like this.

Those of us in the neighborhood know when and where the company Hewlett-Packard (HP) was founded: in the HP Garage at 367 Addison Avenue in Palo Alto in 1937. A few of us know Google started off working in the garage at 232 Santa Margarita, Menlo Park. Fewer still know YouTube started above Amici's Pizza on 3rd Avenue in San Mateo, and perhaps some younger folks know Facebook's first office was above the takeaway Chinese restaurant on Emerson Street.

History is really being made in Silicon Valley every day, and when the landscape is moving so fast and engineers are in high demand, there aren't that many start-ups hiring historians.

THE FUTURE

We know nothing is forever, especially in Silicon Valley. The nature of start-ups is that they grow up or die out. Time is to be savored here. Between long hours of building companies, I've enjoyed driving under the California oaks through the streets of Atherton to Portola Valley, where the deer run in the open meadows. As the sunlight flickers through the twisted branches on my daily drives to see start-ups or VCs, old friends disappear from companies after their four-year stock option vesting schedule has matured while new friends enter my network, renewing my zest for life.

There's been a lot of talk at the dinner parties I've been to in the past few years that the name 'Silicon Valley' isn't relevant anymore! With only two percent of venture capital in 2012 being invested in semiconductor companies and another two percent in hardware, many feel the term 'Silicon' is obsolete and perhaps the Valley should be called 'Web Valley' or 'Internet Valley'. I hope the name doesn't change. The DNA of entrepreneurship is hard-coded into the semiconductor and microprocessor firms like Shockley Semiconductor Laboratory, Fairchild Semiconductor and Intel, which created Silicon Valley. I hope that no one is old enough to forget the brief history of Silicon Valley or indeed bold enough to suggest a name change.

Finally, for all the entrepreneurs that dream of coming to Silicon Valley, be careful what you wish for — sometimes wishes can come true. Even the VCs, as pessimistic as they often seem for having to say no to most deals, are also here in the Valley looking to help entrepreneurs create the next big thing.

Of all the things that Silicon Valley represents, it is hope. As many people think that Silicon Valley is becoming the next Hollywood, I would like to say that if Silicon Valley was a line in a movie, it would be best encapsulated by the words of Morgan Friedman in the movie *The Shawshank Redemption*: 'Hope is a good thing, maybe the best of things, and no good thing ever dies.'

Glossary

The following terms are commonly used in Silicon Valley by both entrepreneurs and VCs:

Acqui-hire The acquisition of a start-up for access to the talent.

Arms Race A competitive situation in which start-ups have become equal.

Bake in Including a piece of technology into a product.

Blind check The amount of money on good faith, without having seen the product, that an investor will write a check for.

Circle the wagons To look into something or undertake further action.

Convertible Note A debt to equity instrument used for financing start-up companies.

Crowdsourcing venture funding refers to raising small amounts of money from a large group of unknown participants. Crowdsourcing funds does not result in participants receiving equity yet often receives a guaranteed pre-ordered product.

Deck An investment presentation, typically in PowerPoint format.

Drinking the Kool Aid Disagreeing with others on how great a start-up company is.

Down Round refers to the valuation of a venture backed company being lower when money is raised compared to the valuation at an earlier stage.

Get behind the numbers is a term used by venture capitalists to describe understanding the financial assumptions that are used in preparing the financial forecasts.

Family and Friends typically refers to the amount of money raised when the start-up is in very early stages. Family and friends typically investments are prior to the seed round and are often exchanged for common stock, not preferred stock in the company.

Financial runway The amount of time a start-up company has, measured in months, given the venture capital funds it has available and the monthly cash burn. For example, a $50,000 burn rate with $500,000 funds available would give a company a financial runway of ten months.

Flat Round refers to the valuation of a venture backed company being the same when money is raised compared to the valuation at an earlier stage.

Friend of the firm A social or professional associate of somebody who works or worked with a venture capital portfolio company.

Hard stop A time when a meeting or phone call must finish.

Hitting your numbers A start-up achieving revenue projections.

Hockey stick The revenue curve that moves from left to right in an upwards direction to chart the revenue rate of a start-up.

Influencers People who are key influencers.

Investment-ready The state of mind and completeness of the investment pitch deck presentation by the start-up founders.

IP Acronym for 'intellectual property'.

Keep their powder dry When a person does not engage in a conversation or negotiation in order to maximize their leverage in future discussions.

Overcooked valuation An excessive valuation, given the stage of the company.

The paperwork The term sheet, convertible notes and other documentation that attorneys prepare for start-ups, which investors require to make an investment.

Pimp your ride When an advisor or third party recommends your company to another company.

Pivot is a Silicon Valley term to describe the changing product and business models a technology start-up company has.

Pony up To put up cash; to deliver the goods.

Reload To make an additional investment in the same company that a previous investment was made in.

Series A The round of venture capital that typically follows the seed round and prior to the Series B round.

Shiny New Thing refers to the newest hottest start-up that the angel ventures chase. It often refers to venture capitalists losing focus on business fundamentals and get blinded by the newest wave of technology start-ups.

Snapchatting Communicating on mobile devices using photos instead of alphabetic text messaging.

Top up the round A maximum amount or ceiling figure for a venture raising.

Uncapped valuation The valuation of a company raising venture capital using a convertible note and which has not priced the round of funding.

Wheelhouse A list of contacts or a reference to a specific business focus.

Zombie fund A venture fund that has not raised an additional fund in the past four years and hence is investing the last of its money. Also known as *the walking dead*, as without further funding it will not be able to operate in the future.

CPSIA information can be obtained at www.ICGtesting.com
Printed in the USA
BVOW02s2009201213

339731BV00003B/57/P